Praise for *The Doctor Crisis*:

"With a unique combination of poetic storytelling, technical mastery, and executive savvy, Dr. Jack Cochran and Charles Kenney offer a design and a call for the learning and leadership we urgently need in health care. In a terrain of political debate too often marked by confusion and reductionist claims, this book brings real wisdom and compassion. It is a must-read for those searching for a route to a new care system." —Donald M. Berwick, MD, President Emeritus and Senior Fellow, Institute for Healthcare Improvement

"The core of this compelling book is the true story of how a dedicated, passionate surgeon took on a leadership role to help turn around a struggling health care organization. Both practical and wise, *The Doctor Crisis* is a must-read for health care leaders everywhere. Cochran and Kenney have managed to capture the discipline and ordinariness of the many small actions and encounters that together produce dramatic organizational change." —Amy C. Edmondson, Novartis Professor of Leadership and Management, Harvard Business School, and author of *Teaming*

"In this time of tumultuous change, physicians have great challenges and wonderful opportunities. Cochran and Kenney effectively make the case for physicians to lead delivery system change, and clearly and persuasively show how physician leadership will be a critical success factor as we build a better health care system for our patients and our communities." —Gary S. Kaplan, MD, Chairman and CEO, Virginia Mason Health System

"The evidence is overwhelming that the American medical system is broken, yet few people have offered the wisdom, grit, and optimism to see a better future and reach for it. Cochran and Kenney have done just that. With extraordinary humanity and solid data, they remind all of us that status should not be confused with leadership. Each of us must learn from other disciplines, live with purpose and transparency, and make sure the joy in medicine is sustained for the next generation." —Nancy L. Snyderman, MD, FACS, NBC News Chief Medical Editor, and Associate Clinical Professor, Head and Neck Surgery, University of Pennsylvania

"Jack Cochran uses his personal experiences to draw important lessons for fundamentally transforming the US health care system. Because failure is truly not an option and the issues transcend mere money to encompass human life and well-being, everyone should read and heed Cochran's profound wisdom." —Jeffrey Pfeffer, Professor of Organizational Behavior, Graduate School of Business, Stanford University

"A compelling portrayal of why physicians must lead and show the way to transformative change in health care. This book should be read by every physician who has lost hope—or is losing hope—in achieving professional fulfillment." —Dennis S. O'Leary, MD, former President, The Joint Commission

"Jack and Charles have written an inspiring piece that illustrates the personal and professional attributes that physicians and health care workers today must embody in order to improve the quality of patient care and to lead innovation within an all-too-fragmented health care service. Textured with moving vignettes from patients and the clinical community, *The Doctor Crisis* challenges physicians to stand up and lead, to take action, and to prioritize learning and evidence-based medicine." —Professor the Lord Ara Darzi, PC, KBE, FRS, Paul Hamlyn Chair of Surgery and Chair of The Institute of Global Health Innovation, Imperial College London

"The vision is compelling and provocative, that physicians and other clinicians should work together to be 'healers-leaders-partners.' The authors compel us with the new work, and also enable us with a rich array of stories, examples, and tools to guide our own personal journeys of growth." —Maureen Bisognano, President and CEO, Institute For Healthcare Improvement

"I have often been inspired by seeing firsthand in Colorado and other places how Dr. Jack Cochran and a great team of physician leaders transformed health care—and I am inspired by the many examples and stories which illustrate how they got started and how they ended up transforming care in a fundamental way. Like many others, I often asked Jack whether he could write these powerful examples down. With Charles Kenny, Jack Cochran has done a fantastic job at preserving the narrative of captivating events as they occurred, while at the same time drawing helpful lessons for system leaders and policy makers alike. A great read for anyone involved in making healthcare better!" —Nicolaus Henke, Global Leader of McKinsey's Healthcare Practice, London

THE DOCTOR CRISIS

How Physicians Can, and Must,
Lead the Way to Better Health Care

Jack Cochran, MD
and
Charles Kenney

PUBLICAFFAIRS
New York

Book Design by BookComp, Inc.

Library of Congress Cataloging-in-Publication Data
Cochran, Jack, author.
    The doctor crisis / Jack Cochran, Charles C. Kenney.—First edition.
        p.   cm.
    Includes index.
    ISBN 978-1-61039-443-7 (hardcover)—ISBN 978-1-61039-444-4
(electronic)
    I. Kenney, Charles, author. II. Title.
    [DNLM: 1. Delivery of Health Care—organization & administra-
tion—United States. 2. Burnout, Professional—United States. 3. Health
Care Reform—organization & administration—United States.
4. Patient-Centered Care—organization & administration—United
States. 5. Physician's Role—United States. 6. Practice Management,
Medical—organization & administration—United States. W 84 AA1]
    RA971
    362.1068—dc23
                                                            2013049312

First Edition
10 9 8 7 6 5 4 3 2 1

Dedication from Jack Cochran, MD

To the Cochran Boys,
Ryan and Taylor
the Lights of my Life . . .

Recognizing the beauty and grace of father and son
relationships with heartfelt gratitude
for the time this life grants us together

Dedication from Charles Kenney

This book is dedicated to the memory of my beloved son

Charles F. Kenney
1987–2012

Belmont Hill School, 2006
Brown University, 2010; Captain, Brown Lacrosse, 2010
1st Lieutenant, United States Marine Corps
S-2, Headquarters Company
7th Marine Regiment
1st Marine Division
I Marine Expeditionary Force

Contents

Authors' Note

In the pages ahead we write a good deal about both the doctor crisis and the Learning Coalition. Here is how we define these terms.

We have superb doctors in the United States. These exceptionally well-trained men and women understand that they are crucial patient advocates. Physicians must accept the responsibility of guiding our nation to a better health care delivery system, but the pathway forward, amid jarring changes in our health care system, is not always clear.

The doctor crisis is the convergence of a complex amalgam of forces preventing primary care and specialty physicians from doing what they most want to do: put their patients first *at every step in the care process every time*. Barriers include overzealous regulation, bureaucracy, the liability burden, reduced reimbursements, and more. As a result, many physicians hold deeply negative views of the medical profession.

Solving the physician crisis is a prerequisite to creating a health care system that is patient-centered, safe, equitable, accessible, and affordable. And we believe that freeing doctors to concentrate on providing excellent care is, by definition, patient-centered.

We use the term "Learning Coalition" to describe an organic gathering of people, organizations, and activities that exist within the fabric of health care today. The Learning Coalition is a dynamic coming together of physicians and other caregivers along with health plans, policy makers, and patients with the core mission of turning the best work *anywhere* into the standard *everywhere*. Ultimately, the Learning Coalition aspires to turn health care into the world's leading learning industry.

Additional note: In a small number of instances, we have changed the names of physicians and patients to protect their privacy.

Preface

We love being doctors because we have the privilege of being able to alleviate suffering, to change lives, and to save lives.

When I traveled to Ecuador to operate on children with a variety of deformities and birth defects, I had the good fortune to meet eight-year-old Antonio Moreno and his father. They had traveled from their remote farming village on foot, then atop a wagon, and finally on a bus—a day-and-a-half journey—to reach the small hospital.

Antonio had been born with a cleft lip. He hated going to school, where other children made fun of his appearance. When I examined Antonio at the hospital, it was clear that he was an ideal candidate for surgery, and we put him on the list. There was such a large number of patients that many who were on the schedule had to wait a couple of days before surgery. Some families were lucky enough to get a small room in a hotel nearby, while others slept on benches outside the hospital.

When Antonio's turn came, my colleagues and I went through a simple routine prior to surgery that includes the anesthesiologist explaining her role and the work as well as the risks. Speaking to Mr. Moreno through an interpreter, the anesthesiologist explained that she was going to put Antonio to sleep and place a breathing tube in his throat. When the surgery was complete, she would let the gas wear off and take out the tube. The anesthesiologist explained that while there are always risks to surgery, she expected it all to go very smoothly.

I watched as the interpreter conveyed this information in Spanish, and it was clear that Mr. Moreno was surprised. He asked, "What risks?"

The anesthesiologist explained that these things were rare but that there could be an infection of some kind or perhaps some excess bleeding, and in extremely rare cases death was possible. As the translation was conveyed, I watched Antonio's father closely. He appeared stricken.

Through the interpreter, Mr. Moreno asked, "He could die?"

Gently, the anesthesiologist explained that it was theoretically possible but extremely unlikely.

Mr. Moreno took his son by the hand and said that they were going back home. When we tried to explain to him that we thought the surgery would go very well, he told the translator, "I am not taking any chance of losing my boy."

Suddenly, the unit grew quite tense. I had performed these surgeries hundreds of times from Nepal to the Philippines to Nicaragua, and I had never before encountered a reaction like this.

But then something amazing happened. Little Antonio led his father by the hand to the far corner of the room, where they spoke in whispers for about fifteen minutes. You could see that it was a highly emotional discussion.

When they were finished talking, the father wept. They emerged from the corner, and Mr. Moreno told us that Antonio said he desperately wanted the surgery. His father told us through the interpreter, "Antonio says he would rather die than live this way."

The only sound in the clinic was that of Antonio's father sobbing. We comforted Mr. Moreno as best we could, settled him in the waiting area, and wheeled Antonio into the operating room. Then we—the clinical team—went to work.

During my career I have performed thousands of surgeries of varying kinds, but having the opportunity to operate on this little boy was one of the greatest blessings of my life. When we were finished and Antonio came in to recovery, his father saw that his son had surely made it through the surgery. Mr. Moreno also saw how beautifully transformed his son's face was. And again Mr. Moreno cried, but this time it was with a profound joy that I will never forget.

I love being a physician. I love it for many reasons, but the main one is because of what I am able to do for people like Antonio. And the incredible thing about being a doctor is that every one of the almost one million physicians in the United States has a similar story—not a cleft lip necessarily but a story in which the physician changed someone's life in a magnificent way. Countless specialists and primary care physicians alike have stories in which they literally *saved* a life—reached in and rescued the patient from the edge of the precipice. Or they saved *many* lives—of children, expectant mothers, and aging grandparents. The joy and satisfaction in those moments for physicians is unlike any other experience.

To reach the point where we can do these things requires years and years of hard work, including the rigor of a heavy science load in college followed by the unrelenting demands of medical school. Academic work combined with clinical training builds the skills that gradually transform the student into a clinician who advances to residency training and fellowship, ranging from three to eight years. Only then comes the great reward: the ability to care for people who *need* you.

This is the heart of the matter. Physicians love being doctors because we have the privilege of being able to calm fears and alleviate suffering—to change and save lives. This is what motivates doctors virtually every single day of their lives. When the structure and culture in which physicians work are well aligned, it is a most rewarding job.

But something has gone wrong in the physician world, and it is urgent that we fix it. Fundamental flaws in our system make it more difficult and less rewarding than ever to be a doctor. A 2012 Physicians Foundation survey found that nearly eight in ten doctors were "somewhat pessimistic or very pessimistic about the future of the medical profession." A report from Harris Interactive, a leading research firm, described the practice of medicine today as "a minefield" where physicians feel burned out and "under assault on all fronts." Mayo Clinic physicians Liselotte N. Dyrbye and Tait D. Shanafelt wrote in a commentary in the *Journal of the American Medical Association* (*JAMA*) that 30–40 percent of physicians in the United States are "experiencing burnout." Dyrbye and Shanafelt note that physicians suffering from burnout "are more likely to report making recent medical errors, score lower on instruments measuring empathy, and plan to retire early and have higher job dissatisfaction, which has been associated with reduced patient satisfaction with medical care and patient adherence to treatment plans."

Never before have physicians been under so much pressure from so many sides. Many physicians feel inundated with administrative matters that prevent them from devoting their full talents to their patients' well-being. Ask doctors about the atmosphere in which they practice, and you often hear words such as "chaos," "conflict," and "dysfunction." *How can a nation transform its health care system when so many physicians feel such deep pessimism about the future of their profession?*

The reality of our situation in the United States is clear. We cannot achieve high-quality, accessible, affordable health care for all unless we solve the doctor crisis. Unless physicians are provided with the team-based support they need to focus on patient care—and are not weighed down by work that other team members can do—progress will stall. And lest anyone read into our view that we are being overly physician-centric by focusing on the doctor crisis, we strongly believe that freeing doctors to concentrate on providing excellent care is, by definition, patient-centered. In fact, when the question "what do physicians want?" is asked, the answer is clear. Physicians want the team support to be able to give their patients the time, attention, and care they need. That is what drives the great majority of doctors in our nation, and while the crisis is most acute within primary care, it applies across the specialties as well. As Dr. Jay Crosson, vice president of Professional Satisfaction, Care Delivery, and Payment at the American Medical Association, observes, "Taking physician satisfaction seriously does not mean giving physicians anything they want, but it should mean creating an environment where physicians are always able to put patients first."

And that is the heart of the doctor crisis. Far too often, physicians are prevented from putting their patients first—ahead of administrative hassles, finances, insurance company demands, regulations, and more. These barriers nearly all make sense when one looks at them from a point of view *other than the patient,* but if we put the patient's well-being ahead of every other consideration, then it is clear that these barriers must be breached.

Why a book focused on doctors at a time when the language of health care reform is about being patient-centered? Because my coauthor Charles Kenney and I believe that *one of the most patient-centered actions we can take is to fix the doctor crisis in our country.* Solving this problem is a prerequisite to creating a health care system that is patient-centered, safe, equitable, accessible, and affordable—in other words, to achieving the health care system that we so urgently need in the United States.

Solving the doctor crisis means removing the many barriers between doctors and their patients. But it also means demanding that physicians step up and take stronger leadership roles *on behalf of their patients.* The bright young men and women who grind their way through medical school and years of training did not do so to check boxes on a form, engage in verbal duels with insurance companies, and spend two to three hours on paperwork. For generations, physicians were primarily healers. Yet in our complex world, they are tasked with broader responsibilities. They must become stronger leaders and better partners. In the United States, patients, families, and communities struggle with uneven quality and access and with inequity and rising costs. A variety of stakeholders can contribute to solving these challenges, but physicians have a disproportionate impact on these issues and a disproportionate responsibility to take on these challenges. Unfortunately, there are too many instances where physicians have served as barriers to change rather than as agents of change. Some doctors are most comfortable on a pedestal. But the great majority of physicians want what is best for their patients, and this drives an increasing number of doctors to actively work for dynamic improvement. Physicians are part of the problem in some places, but they are also essential to the solution *everywhere*.

Just as physicians have a broader responsibility than ever before, so too does our society have a responsibility to support physicians by emphasizing the preservation and enhancement of their professional careers. We need to liberate doctors from the work that others can capably handle to allow physicians to focus on providing the best care possible. Preserving the professional dignity and idealism of physicians and enhancing their career experience can play a major role in achieving a patient-centered system.

The physician crisis in our country is too often overlooked in policy discussions about future pathways for improving care delivery. The health care improvement movement in the United States is robust and growing. It includes clinicians, administrators, policy makers, and others seeking to create a system whose hallmarks are access, quality, and affordability. Too often, however, policy makers and activists within the improvement movement target physicians as obstacles to improvement—as stubborn, immovable barriers to change. And this is sometimes true. But the time is long overdue for recognizing that the physician crisis is real, urgent, and solvable.

Jack Cochran, MD

PART I
Miracles, Urgency

A Higher Calling

1

A Kind of Miracle

The Beauty of American Medicine

Our biggest fear obviously, besides survival, . . . was that they'd be paralyzed.

When the ultrasound revealed that Emily Stark was pregnant with twins, she and her husband Jim experienced that rare joy bestowed upon first-time parents. The result of a subsequent ultrasound, however, was crushing: the twins were not separate; they were conjoined. When the doctor broke the news—stating solemnly "they're joined"—Emily and Jim wept.

Most of their urgent questions were unanswerable at that point. The issue of survival loomed over all, but there was no doubt that Jim and Emily would proceed with the birthing process. These were their precious babies, and they wanted desperately to give them life.

The birth presented exceptionally rare challenges. It is often difficult to get a baby out of the mother's uterus, and getting two babies out can be quite complex indeed. But the birth of two babies—physically joined together—presented complexities of a magnitude greater still. The geometry alone was immensely challenging. The obstacles were many—managing the girls' airways, dealing with angles of their bodies, and more.

A C-section was scheduled, and Emily was admitted to Saint Joseph's Hospital in Denver with a simple hope: that the girls would survive. Dr. Brad McDowell, a plastic and reconstructive surgeon, assembled the medical team (including Jack Cochran) who would treat the girls. The three leaders of the team included Dr. McDowell; Dr. Michael Handler, a neurosurgeon; and Dr. Joseph Janik, a pediatric surgeon.

McDowell and the team leaders agreed that they had to be ready to separate the girls immediately after birth in case something should go terribly awry. The physicians' hope was that they could successfully deliver the babies and then have time to further explore how to separate them—if that was what the parents wished.

McDowell described the scene. "We put together an obstetrical and neonatal team, and we were already pulling together a broader team for possible separation. We were all there, about thirty of us in the room for the birth around 6 or 7 o'clock in the evening. We didn't know what the situation would be. Would one child be in distress and have to be separated right away? We knew from the X-rays they were joined at the spine, which was pretty serious."

As tricky as the birth was, it went smoothly thanks to the planning and skill of the obstetrical and neonatal teams. It is difficult to overstate the skill and passion with which these team members worked—physicians and nurses. The delivery was likely the most challenging any team member had ever encountered, yet every physician and nurse involved performed to the highest possible standards of excellence. It was magnificent to see.

The girls—Lexi and Syd—were brought into the world on March 9, 2001, two months shy of their due date. Each weighed four pounds.

"The children both had some respiratory issues," recalled McDowell, "but they were okay, and they were taken immediately to the neonatal nursery, wheeled down the hallway past the family where there was a lot of crying and a lot of smiles."

But just hours after the birth, a problem was identified by the surgical team. Doctors discovered that Syd did not have an opening connecting her intestines to the outside of her body. Without surgical intervention, there was a possibility that the obstruction within the intestinal tract would lead to sepsis and death. The situation required urgent surgery—an emergency colostomy—just twelve hours after the birth. A small team of surgeons, anesthesiologists, plastic surgeons, and neonatologists mobilized for the early Saturday morning surgery that successfully solved the intestinal obstruction.

While the birth and the urgent surgery were rare challenges, they were nothing like what lay ahead.

Conjoined twins are exceptionally rare. In the United States, for every one million births about four are conjoined. Scientists believe that during the first two weeks of pregnancy an embryo splits nearly in half rather than completely. Parts of the embryo remain attached.

Jim and Emily Stark, both thirty-one years old, had a decision to make: Should the girls be surgically separated, or should they be raised as they were? Raising them as they were would be difficult, of course, but certainly not impossible—and it would remove some of the frightening risks associated with surgical separation.

Before the parents could make the decision, they needed to know the medical facts. Did the girls share a common bladder or bowel? How comingled were the complex series of nerves that controlled so many functions of their bodies, from waste to reproduction? Could they be separated and both survive? If they did survive, would they ever be able to walk? Would they be paralyzed? Would they be able to have children?

"We could keep them forever," Emily said, "or we can try to make their lives better with the potential that we may not be bringing them home" (*Denver Post*).

The possibility of separation surgery triggered profound anxiety. Jim Stark had said early on that one of his most precious wishes was to be able to play sports with his girls when they were older. "I envisioned running in the park with my kids and playing baseball and playing hockey," said Jim. "That's not going to happen."

Jim heard physicians telling them that the worst-case scenario was "waist-down paralysis . . . for life. . . . We're ready for paralysis. We're ready for . . . [a] colostomy. But I don't think you can ever be ready to not have one of them."

The parents had another decision to make: Who would do the surgery? Were there surgical superstars out there somewhere in the health care universe? Should they go to the Mayo Clinic, Johns Hopkins, or the Cleveland Clinic? They considered a variety of specialists around the world but decided in the end that they were comfortable with the excellent team in their hometown of Denver. They trusted the men and women at Kaiser Permanente (KP) and Denver Children's Hospital. KP was one of the best-integrated health care systems in the United States, and Denver Children's Hospital was renowned for quality. One of the great things about health care in the United States is that the level of talent is world-class at so many major medical centers throughout the nation. In America, there is no monopoly on medical brilliance.

Many aspects of the case were highly unusual, of course. One was the size of the clinical team. The twenty-two doctors in total were from both KP Colorado and Denver Children's Hospital. This level of collaboration was essential for a successful separation, yet it is rarely seen in today's health care system. Health care at the time—and largely still today—was siloed.

Yet this work required silos to be broken down. It required the combined efforts of the Colorado Permanente Medical Group and the physicians and staff at Denver Children's Hospital, where the separation surgery would be done. The successful collaboration painted a portrait of U.S. health care at its finest, demonstrating integration of services and cooperation among a large team of highly skilled physicians and staff.

The surgical team, led by Brad McDowell along with Drs. Joseph Janik and Michael Handler, coordinated the separation plan. The delivery and intensive care team was managed by Peter Hulac, neonatology, and Robert McDuffie, obstetrics. The anesthesia team of Drs. Theresa Youtz and Patti Coughlin also played a central role, managing the complex and delicate job of providing anesthesia to two joined babies. Multiple other physicians and nurses in orthopedic surgery, urology, pediatrics, and plastic surgery were also intimately involved in the successful care of the twins.

This was a wonderful example of American medicine at its best. Superbly trained clinicians working as a highly functional team—doctors, nurses, pharmacists, and technicians all working in a coordinated way under steady, inspired physician leadership.

"We held a series of meetings over a period of months because we had decided that the optimal time to separate them was at seven months, which gave us time to do a great deal of research and put an excellent plan together," explained McDowell. "At our meetings we talked everything through: What did the neurosurgeons need? How about urology and pediatric surgery? What were the challenges each faced, and how could we overcome them? We got clarity on what information, studies, instrumentation, and time everyone would need. And we began to put an order together for the operation—what exactly would happen when and who would do it."

In preparation for the separation surgery, the doctors performed multiple imaging tests to define the anatomy of the Stark twins. This included a three-dimensional CT scan from which a precise anatomic model of the spine was created. This allowed the team to see and touch a correct anatomic model of the twins' conjoined spine, which was invaluable to surgical planning. The team also reviewed and discussed the medical literature available on conjoined twins' separation. Each specialty involved—pediatrics, pediatric surgery, plastic surgery, urology, obstetrics, neurosurgery, anesthesiology, neonatology, and nursing—engaged in close communication, all the while building a coordinated strategy for the surgery. Each team member refined and clarified what would be required for a successful separation.

As doctors prepared for surgery, they were encouraged by the knowledge that the girls had separate hearts, kidneys, livers, and intestines. These were critical indices suggesting a high likelihood of survival. However, the twins did have a significant shortage of skin. A successful separation would require a greater amount of skin to close the surgical wounds. Thus, months before the planned separation, a team of plastic surgeons placed multiple tissue expanders in each girl's back. This would allow the surgeons to slowly stretch the skin, creating the additional skin needed at separation.

The ongoing tissue expansion created another challenge for the team: How would the girls sleep with these large tissue expanders in place? In addition, doctors were concerned that prolonged pressure on the skin over the expanders could damage or kill the tenuous skin. The problem was solved by providing an air mattress, allowing the girls to sleep on a pressure-free surface and avoid injury to the expanded skin.

During one of the regularly scheduled surgical team meetings, the team decided to perform a full dress rehearsal for the separation surgery. On the Saturday two weeks prior to operation, the team gathered for a rehearsal using two dolls attached back-to-back with Velcro as stand-ins for Syd and Lexi. Working in the operating room (OR), the team laid out a step-by-step plan for the operation.

"We thought the best way to really solidify the plan was to go through it in rehearsal," says McDowell. "We walked through every part of the whole procedure with the dolls. The first step was to put them to sleep, and then we went through who would do what first and then the exact sequence. We knew there would be issues along the way, and we talked through what they might be."

The team worked through the entire procedure from beginning to end and created a written timeline of the anticipated events. Every one of these experienced people was entirely focused on those two dolls—on getting the girls through this not just so they would survive but so they could *thrive and enjoy rich, long lives.* This was the care team's mission.

October 9, 2001, dawned gray and raw in Denver. It was a day of drizzle, flurries, and slick roads. At 7:30 a.m. in Denver Children's Hospital, Jim and Emily prayed over their tiny daughters before the babies were wheeled into the OR, where twenty-two doctors, scrubbed and gowned, stood ready. The physicians in this case, supported by a team of nurses and technicians, shared hundreds of years of clinical experience, yet none had ever attempted—never mind accomplished—the procedure in front of them. What happened in the OR over the next sixteen hours would determine in so many ways the paths of these babies' and their parents' lives.

That morning, men and women in scrubs moved purposefully toward the OR. Everyone knew about the momentous event that was about to take place. Surgical team members had arrived for work that morning in the dark, and daylight would come and go while they remained in the OR until night had fallen.

Surgeons often get tense before they go to work, and this is a very good thing. It tends to heighten their senses and sharpen their focus. There was, of course, an added dose of anxiety on this morning.

Jim and Emily gathered together with surgeons, the anesthesiologists, and relatives in the surgical holding area. It was here that the girls were anesthetized. While the parents had accompanied the girls into the OR, they left before the procedure began. They were counseled by physicians not to watch the operation even on the closed-circuit monitor where other clinicians were viewing it.

Jim Stark would later express his fears. "Our biggest fear obviously, besides survival, which can be a problem in any operation, was that they'd be paralyzed. . . . I think our biggest fear was their spinal cord and their spinal column were conjoined and attached. So I think when we got down to it, . . . separating that part out and what nerves went to which girl, were there any cross-overs? Was . . . Sydney's spine controlling Lexi's legs or vice versa?"

The next sixteen hours were a model of orchestration and precision. The teams followed their rehearsal plan, and each time a challenging or unanticipated situation arose, the specialists huddled, discussed it, and came to a consensus decision. One practical step helped the team tell the girls apart at all points. Because they were joined their four legs were tangled together quite a bit, and it was not always easy to tell which were Lexi's and which were Syd's. So the surgeons simply "drew an 'S' on Syd's feet and an 'L' on Lexi's." Each girl had her own surgical team, and to eliminate any doubt each team wore different-colored surgical hats.

McDowell made the initial incision, dividing the soft tissue all the way down to the bone, at which point orthopedic surgeons and then neurosurgeons stepped in. A significant challenge came with the task of identifying and separating the girls' internal organs in and around the perineal region, an area adjacent to the vagina and anus involving a variety of critical human functions. Yet another hurdle was the task of separating the babies' spinal nerves and bones.

Approximately eight hours into the surgery, Syd and Lexi were placed in the prone position so that surgeons could complete the separation. As the hours ticked by, doctors separated the bones, muscles, and nerves that the girls shared. Surgeons also separated their intestinal and reproductive tracts. In the final hours, surgeons focused on the spinal cord—more specifically the nerve fibers of the dural sac, a membrane that encases the spinal cord.

A Denver TV station filmed the operation and broadcast various segments. A reporter writing about the broadcast noted that "the most jarring moment for the lay observer is . . . when a tap-tap-tap sound is heard and the doctor uses 'the medical equivalent of a hammer and chisel' to separate the babies' spines."

After almost twelve hours of surgery, the final tap on the spine occurred to separate the twins. In the OR, the plastic surgeons moved in to take on the task of mobilizing and providing adequate soft-tissue coverage of all the previously repaired vital structures. They examined the stretched skin carefully to make sure to select only healthy, viable skin. McDowell led this work, and within about three hours the new skin was in place on both Syd and Lexi. And suddenly there they were, two separated, beautiful little babies.

After a brief moment when everyone realized what had been accomplished, a cheer arose from the doctors and staff that echoed off the OR walls. (In an unexpectedly whimsical moment, the closed incision for Syd was in the shape of an L, while the closed incision on Lexi was in the shape of an S.)

The girls were rolled down the hallway in separate beds to the ICU. The hallway was lined with family members, parents front and center. Everybody was laughing and smiling, and at the same time it seemed that nearly everybody was crying.

The twins had a generally unremarkable postoperative course. They remained in the hospital for eight days. Each twin had a separate bed in which to recover from the surgery. On about the third postoperative day, Syd and Lexi were briefly placed together in the same bed. It was the first time in their lives they had seen each other face to face. They cried continuously until they were separated again.

Brad McDowell followed the girls throughout the healing process as the years passed and Syd and Lexi grew and thrived. "I ran into the mom one day a few years ago," recalls McDowell, "and the girls were so active and energetic and running around—and so alive! And their mom laughed and said to me 'I wish sometimes you'd hook them back together again!'"

As McDowell reflects on the operation, he says that being part of it was exciting and deeply gratifying. There was much stress and worry, of course, "but it really is a fulfilling thing to look back on. And the truth is that everybody lived happily ever after."

2

The Other Side
of the Miracle

Failure Is Not an Option

The reality of our health care system is that it contains men and women with years of excellent clinical training who are capable of performing miracles—as was shown with the Stark twins. These medical professionals coordinate to solve complex problems and engage in superb teamwork—all focused on what is best for the patient. And it works! It not only works, but it is also inspiring and brilliant and is one of the finest things we do in the United States. Yet at the same time, throughout the country health care is unreliable, plagued by unnecessary variation and extensive waste. The Institute of Medicine suggests that as much as one-third of the $2.9 trillion spent annually on health care in the United States may be wasted.

The dichotomy is very familiar to those of us who have worked at Kaiser Permanente (KP) for twenty years or more. We know firsthand how effective the KP culture and structure can be. KP's integrated system is built on the relationship between accountable multispecialty medical groups and a nonprofit hospital system and health plan. KP's philosophy, structure, and incentives are aligned and enable all staff members to work collaboratively to maximize our members' total health. The system works very simply: a patient signs up to become a KP member and have KP provide insurance and care. The Kaiser Foundation Health Plan provides the member with comprehensive health benefits, and the Permanente Medical Groups provide or arrange medical services.

Our approach has worked remarkably well for decades. But we are fallible human beings, and we recognize in our own history an object lesson in the complex challenges that face so many health care organizations today. The mid-1990s in the KP Colorado region was a period rich with lessons for improvement. During this time, patients experienced great frustration in simply trying to make an appointment or get advice from a nurse. Frequently, patients were placed on hold for long periods. Too often, when they did get through they were unable to get the appointments they wanted with their own doctor. The same organization that could coordinate with Denver Children's Hospital to help facilitate an astonishingly delicate operation—one that provided two girls with wonderful, normal lives—was the same organization that just a few years earlier struggled to competently answer phones and set up appointments! The problems ran deeper than the call center—so deep that the physician turnover rate accelerated as physician satisfaction rates plunged. We experienced significant membership losses, twelve thousand in all leaving the KP Colorado system. And on top of it all, KP Colorado suffered significant financial shortfalls.

How could this happen in the same system that was capable of performing clinical miracles? How did the organization responsible for the miraculous Stark surgery perfect something that it would do once in a lifetime and yet bungle something that it does thousands of times every day—answer phone calls to schedule patient appointments?

Look around the country. How do we explain the epidemic of patients falling and injuring themselves even in our finest hospitals? Why is the patient transition from hospital to home often so poorly done that many patients wind up back in the hospital weeks, days, or even hours later? How do we explain the waste, something approaching $750 billion of health care money every year? Why are the vast majority of patients with diabetes not getting the simple treatments they need to remain healthy and out of hospitals? Why are millions of patients harmed every year in hospitals? Why do thousands of patients die yearly from medical errors? Why is our system so expensive—double what any other industrial nation pays? How is it that so many smart people participate in and preside over a system that is so dysfunctional?

We *can* fix this, and we owe it to every family in the United States to do so. The cost of health care and the burden of caring for loved ones who are ill are mounting pressures on families, often reaching the point of being unsustainable. The average cost of health care per family in the United States exceeds $20,000 per year when you calculate the real costs—including employer contribution, insurance premiums, and copayments.

The American Dream is under siege, and health care is a leading barbarian at the gate. Health care is the central domestic challenge of our time. It is not only harming families and choking our economy but it also threatens our national well-being and economic viability. The health care crisis in the United States impacts families, businesses, communities, governments, and the economy as a whole. And our response to the threat is inadequate. We need to create an inflection point whereby physicians throughout our country stand up and acknowledge that the approach we have used for many years no longer works. Physicians responsible for the well-being of their patients must acknowledge the urgent need for a new pathway forward. This new pathway leads to greater quality, access, and affordability. It leads to a new place where much of the work placed on physicians' shoulders can be accomplished by effective clinical teams working closely together. That is why it is so critical that physicians embrace care delivery as a team effort.

The new pathway for patient care leads to a place where the redistribution of work means that physicians concentrate on tasks that only they are capable of and trained to do and that they perform little if any of the work that others are capable of and trained to do. The new pathway enables doctors to spend more time with their patients, even as the patient population in primary care expands. The new pathway leads us to a point where work-life balance for physicians enables them to experience that profound sense of satisfaction of being a healer. The great majority of physicians are driven by a noble mission. Yet in the fog of confusion, regulation, and overall dysfunction that so often marks our current system, it is often difficult for doctors to see that mission as clearly as they once did. Physician-satisfaction levels in the United States today are alarmingly low.

The iconic physician Jonas Salk put it this way: "Our greatest responsibility is to be good ancestors." This is a wonderful description of the lifelong responsibility of physicians that recognizes that what matters most is the legacy. It is an approach to delivering care that embodies all we can do for our patients.

The most effective way to be good ancestors is to *learn our way out of this crisis.* We have a responsibility to identify the very best practices for quality, efficiency, and cost control; package them so that they are easily spread; and share them with organizations throughout the country. We must realign incentives and spread the kind of knowledge and best practices that improve quality and efficiency and drive premiums down so that the American people can afford this critical aspect of the American Dream. Health care must become the finest learning industry in the world, and today it stands miles away from that goal.

In spite of impressive advances in patient care, we still struggle with foundational elements, including quality, equity, access, and affordability. And we continue to experience uneven clinical results and widespread unwarranted variation in care. We face immense challenges ranging from the supply and sustainability of primary care physicians to the shortage of nurses and other health care workers to baby boomers entering Medicare.

Dr. Arnie Milstein from Stanford and professor Steve Shortell from Berkeley are among our leading health care visionaries in the United States. Milstein is a professor of medicine at Stanford University and the leader of the Stanford Clinical Excellence Research Center. Shortell serves as distinguished professor of health policy and management professor of organizational behavior at the University of California Berkeley Haas School of

Business. They coauthored an article in *JAMA* (October 10, 2012), writing that

> The United States needs to slow its rate of growth in inflation-adjusted per capita health spending by 2.5 percentage points annually without sacrificing health or slowing biomedical technology advances.
>
> The consequences of failure may include shifting of funding away from resources for elementary and high school education, infrastructure (such as highways), and basic science research, as well as weakening the global competitiveness and financial health of US workers and their employers.

Let's consider this for a moment. Two of the most respected thinkers in health care say that the consequences of our failure to make the necessary change to the U.S. health care system include *"weakening the global competitiveness and financial health of US workers."*

So what do we need to do to fix the problem? We certainly cannot legislate our way out of the problem— we must *learn* our way out. We must learn to provide a much higher quality of care at a lower price. In short, we share the view of many health care leaders that improved quality will ultimately be the most powerful force for controlling costs.

Milsetein and Shortell write that in the longer term "one approach lies upstream—the prevention of disease by mitigating underlying environmental, social, and behavioral health risks. The most immediate progress is likely to come downstream from innovations that safely and compassionately lower health spending by reducing the cost of hospitalization for all patients and its unplanned occurrence for the 5% of individuals who incur half of health care expenditures in the United States."

The challenge is clear: we must measurably improve access, affordability, and quality while simultaneously addressing the 30 percent of costs that constitute waste. And as others have said, you don't take more than $700 billion out of a system without anyone noticing.

Len Nichols is a professor of health policy and the director of the Center for Health Policy Research and Ethics at George Mason University. He conveys a message similar to Milsetein and Shortell, using a dynamic analogy to characterize the urgent need to transform health care in the United States. Nichols describes it as our "twenty-first century version of a Sputnik moment," referring to the Soviet Union's successful launch of a satellite that orbited Earth, beating the United States in the space race.

"The scale of the problem we face—how do you pull 30 cents out of this dollar? That scale is equivalent to Sputnik," says Nichols. "It is equivalent to a moon shot. It is equivalent to the biggest thing we've ever done."

As a child in the late 1950s, Nichols heard about Sputnik from his grandmother, and he remembered her fear of the Russians. "My grandmother's fear spread across the country"—a fear that was real and palpable in America at the time. But Americans are resilient, and there was a resolve that Nichols's grandmother and millions of others had. That "resolve also spread across the country and by God we beat their ass. By God, we came together and we did it. How'd we do that? *Because we believed we had to!* Because we faced a threat, a threat not unlike what" we now face.

During a Permanente Executive Leadership Summit in 2012, Nichols made clear that he was not done with his space analogies as they related to health care. He compared the current health care situation not only to Sputnik but also to the plight of Apollo 13, as depicted in the film starring Tom Hanks.

"The tagline everybody talks about is, *'Houston, we have a problem,'*" recalled Nichols. "But what people sometimes remember when you think about it is the best line from the movie actually was when Gene Kranz, the leader of the team, the Ed Harris character, comes together in that room of a thousand smart geeks and basically says, 'We gotta get those boys down, and failure is not an option.'"

And failure was not an option because "they're part of a community. They're part of a family. They are in this together. And by God, they got 'em back. By God, they got 'em back. Now it's not easy. Remember when he put the equipment in a room and said, 'This is what they have up there.' And you've got to show how they can do it with this bunch of plastic and whatever crap they had, duct tape. It looked like my back yard. . . . And they put together those valves and connections that made that return journey possible."

WE ARE THE GEEKS WITH DUCT TAPE

During his presentation, Nichols looked out over an audience that consisted of what we call the Learning Coalition—doctors and administrators from KP, Atrius Health, Virginia Mason Medical Center, Mayo Clinic, Cleveland Clinic, the Institute for Healthcare Improvement, the Department of Defense, HealthPartners, Jonkoping County Sweden, Britain's National Health Service, and many, many more.

Speaking to these early adopters of efforts to reform health care, Nichols declared, "You know, the role of the prophet in history is not just to say, 'What's wrong? What's going on?' It's to imagine a better future. You have to tell us how that future can come to be; otherwise, we're probably not going to make it."

What he was telling us essentially is that we—this amorphous yet growing Learning Coalition—are the geeks with the duct tape! And we have the responsibility to do the equivalent in health care to getting those astronauts safely back to Earth.

The speed of learning and innovation in health care is much too slow, and it is urgent that we fix it. And we have the ability to do so; we can create that inflection point whereby health care becomes an enabler of a better future. It is already happening every day among the Learning Coalition. The question is, how do we accelerate it? How do we share it? How do we make it go *much faster*? How can we become as nimble and passionate and determined and as successful as those wonderful geeks in Apollo 13?

Indeed, what do we mean exactly by "the Learning Coalition"? First, the Learning Coalition is *not* a formal membership organization. It does not have a central office, staff, board, or website. It is far more organic than that.

When we talk about the Learning Coalition, we are describing people, organizations, and activities that *exist within the fabric* of health care today. There are places around the country where the coalition's presence is robust, while there are many other places where it barely has a heartbeat. Yet the coalition has become a growing force whereby physicians and other caregivers come together to identify and solve problems that are common throughout health care.

At its core, the goal of the Learning Coalition is to turn the best work *anywhere* into the standard *everywhere*.

Dr. Donald Berwick, former head of the Centers for Medicare and Medicaid Services (CMS) for the United States, defines what the Learning Coalition has already accomplished: "It's not hard to describe the health care system we want; it's not even hard to find it. . . . Among the gems and the jewels throughout our country . . . lie answers; not theoretical ones, real ones, where we can go and visit these organizations and see how good they are."

The Learning Coalition can be found in the safety improvements at Johns Hopkins, in presurgical huddles taking place from New England Baptist to Intermountain Health, in the Optimal Diabetes Measure at HealthPartners in Minnesota, in the work of the Pacific Business Group on Health, in the safety initiatives of the Lucian Leape Institute, in the educational conferences convened by the Institute for Healthcare Improvement and the Alliance of Community Health Plans, in the Dartmouth Atlas, in the work of grassroots medical school student organizations such as Primary Care Progress, and in the efforts of the Patient Centered Primary Care Collaborative. The Learning Coalition pulses with life in the form of the Institute for Healthcare Improvement's Open School. The Open School is defined by the institute as providing "students of medicine, nursing, public health, pharmacy, health administration, dentistry, and other allied health professions with the opportunity to learn about quality improvement and patient safety at no charge." The mission is as ambitious as it is noble: "To advance health care improvement and patient safety competencies in the next generation of health professionals worldwide."

In just five years, the Open School has proven to be one of the most popular programs anywhere in the Learning Coalition, with 613 chapters in sixty-three countries and 110,194 students and residents having completed an Open School online course.

And the Learning Coalition can be found marbled throughout KP, where our integrated health system, with hospitals, employed physicians, and a health plan work together to ensure access, quality, and affordability across the continuum of care.

The Learning Coalition flourishes at KP and many other locations yet struggles elsewhere. Too many physicians and other health care professionals today remain on the sidelines, apart from the Learning Coalition. The gravitational pull of health care leaders who are unable or unwilling to propel themselves and their organizations forward into the new health care universe is an enormous detriment to the spread of innovation in health care reform in the United States. They do not yet recognize that we have no choice as a nation but to simultaneously pursue the goals of better patient care at a lower cost.

Don Berwick has observed that "Most doctors, nurses, technicians, managers, and others—even executives and boards of directors—will not describe their workplaces as anything like new, refreshed, learning organizations. More likely they will find days filled not with continual improvement but rather with continual fights to stabilize, to get through the latest storm, or to simply survive the day's work. Of course, they care about what they do—most care deeply—but they lack leverage, optimism, and opportunity to change their work. Instead, they just do their work. When they do find a chance to make an improvement, it will likely be local, personal, and, too often, evanescent. The status quo system is the default."

Maureen Bisognano, the CEO at the Institute for Healthcare Improvement, has seen huge progress during her three decades in health care. But she has also seen—particularly recently—a profoundly disturbing pattern in some places:

> Just as it is thrilling to see so many provider organizations moving rapidly in [a positive] direction, it is discouraging to see others failing to find the energy and vision for a new way forward.
>
> As I travel the country I see a disturbing fault line that separates health care organizations. There are many organizations that have a clear sense that a new way forward is necessary, and they're working feverishly on that. But I also see other organizations that have no plan and no real sense of where they are going.
>
> I see a kind of segmentation that is unfortunate. Some health care leaders are frightened about trying to look at all three parts of the Triple Aim. They're frightened about having the conversation with employers and physicians. And they're thinking, "if I can just hang on for a few more years I'll be okay."
>
> They are hanging on, clinging to the status quo.

Hanging on, clinging to the status quo. None of the geeks feverishly working to get the astronauts safely back to Earth were just *hanging on.* Nobody working to beat Sputnik was just *hanging on.* And yet in health care in the United States today, it too often seems that the hangers on outnumber the members of the Learning Coalition.

Dr. Gary Kaplan, the CEO at the Virginia Mason Medical Center in Seattle, sees it this way: "In the final analysis this is a big-time cultural change. We're looking for opportunities to lead that change. The losers will be organizations who cannot change, who are unable to redesign in ways that allow us to move forward and meet the needs of our society, in improving quality and safety and lowering costs. The prospect of losing needs to be an incentive to get on board. You don't need to be a champion, but you cannot be an impediment to moving forward."

3

Healer, Leader, Partner

Which stakeholder—physicians, hospitals, health plans, or others—will lead delivery system transformation? We believe it must be physicians.

Physicians hold the keys to making health care in the United States truly great. This is not in any way meant to degrade the importance of nurses, technicians, pharmacists, medical assistants, administrators, and others. Yet the disproportionate physician influence means that we can achieve our goal of a transformed health care system *only* if physicians provide meaningful patient-centered leadership.

Change for doctors is nothing new. The role of the physician in our society has evolved significantly over time, but now we are at a critical moment when our society must ask doctors to accelerate the speed of that evolution as never before. We must ask doctors to do something different than what many have been doing, something that may be outside their comfort zones. *We ask them to become accountable leaders—leaders with the* vision and courage to lead the transformation of health care in the United States. We ask them to become the kind of leaders who consider *hanging on to the status quo,* as Maureen Bisognano put it, to be a betrayal of their patients. Too many doctors resist meaningful change and prefer the status quo while they resist becoming excellent team players. But the status quo in health care is a prescription for failure, and we need physician leadership and teamwork to improve the quality, access, and affordability of care in our nation.

What defines a physician? What is his or her responsibility in our society? We know that physicians routinely perform feats of clinical brilliance—as we saw with the Stark twins' surgery. As patients, we feel the visceral sense of comfort from the competence and compassion of our doctors. We know that when the exam room door closes, we are in a private place of trust. We know of our doctors' profound devotion to healing our ills and calming our fears.

We ask the question *"What is a physician?"* because the doctor's role has evolved over time, with a particularly rapid evolutionary acceleration in recent years, and many physicians feel confused or resentful about the direction that health care has taken. The deal is not what they signed up for. It is not only the ever-expanding volume and complexity of the clinical work that they face. Far too many physicians also find themselves working amid circumstances characterized by chaos and waste, being encouraged to practice defensive medicine, and being pressured by excessive regulation and hectoring insurance companies.

These circumstances can change rapidly if physicians, administrators, and patients align behind a new pathway forward. The power of patients to affect change is immense. Already, millions of patients and their family members actively participate in the Information Age of medicine via the Internet. They engage in online communities specific to their health conditions. They research a wide variety of conditions in popular and academic journals. They maintain their own medical records, and much more.

THE EVOLUTION OF THE PHYSICIAN'S ROLE

The physician's evolution requires shifting from an Industrial Age model of care to an Information Age model of care. In the Industrial Age model, the doctor focused on illness. He (nearly always *he*), worried about each patient, one at a time, making his clinical decisions in conditions of virtually total autonomy. There were wonderful aspects to this care. It was often highly localized and intensely personal. There was a warmth to it that was derived from a sense of a physician's responsibility to family, friends, and community.

But there was no information technology, there were few sophisticated diagnostic techniques, and there was a limited use of other team members able to provide highly valuable care. Doctors knew what they knew. There were fewer sources of information and knowledge about new medical techniques, and innovation spread at a glacial pace.

In the Information Age, physicians take responsibility not just for individual patients but also for managing populations of patients—those with diabetes, for example—to make sure patients are fully up to date on all of the treatments and measures that improve their overall condition. Information Age physicians skillfully use electronic medical records, clinical registries—data on large numbers of patients and the internet—to help determine the most effective treatments and provide a great deal of care outside the doctor's office. In the Information Age, metrics are central to delivering the best care to patients, many of whom engage in deep research related to their conditions on a nearly endless variety of websites dedicated to diseases, cures, and treatments. Too often, the question in health care for physicians is how many patients you can see today. But in the Information Age, the better question is how many patients' problems you can solve today—and this speaks to the role of physician as leader in the Information Age.

It is not just physicians who are operating within the Information Age. Increasingly, it is, as we have noted, patients as well. The Information Age model requires disruptive innovation to the health care system by holding doctors responsible for all six of the Institute of Medicine's essential elements of quality care: that it is *safe, timely, effective, efficient, equitable,* and *patient-focused.*

But is this fair? Is it reasonable to ask doctors to become something more than they have been? Some physicians chafe at the Information Age model. Most physicians already feel overwhelmed—understandably so. They are asked to do too much in a system that too often thwarts their efforts as much as it enables them.

We have no illusions about how difficult change in health care can be, especially among doctors. Dr. Gene Lindsey, former CEO of Atrius Health in Boston, has worked diligently in recent years to shift the culture of his organization, and he has found this to be exceedingly difficult work.

"There is so much anxiety in the physician community," says Lindsey. "Adaptive change is enormous work. It means giving up things we thought were bedrock."

He cites the example of a physician who is a true expert in his clinical field and then must go through *lean* training—learning a variety of lean management tools and methods to improve quality, safety, and efficiency. "So you go from being completely competent in an area to being a novice in a new domain. There are a lot of heated conversations."

Many doctors argue that the essence of their job is clinical: that a good doctor focuses on the condition with which a patient presents and then uses her or his skill and training to cure the problem. And many physicians will always cling to that definition exclusively, insisting that matters such as access, cost, and such are better left to administrators and policy makers. *But isn't that what we've been doing for at least the past few decades?* And look where it's gotten us. In the years to come, that definition will seem as outdated as a late-night physician house call. For a doctor to focus exclusively on being a great clinician, we must believe that everything in the realm of health care that now affects our patients is precisely as it should be or will be fixed by people other than physicians. And *nobody* believes that.

HEALER-LEADER-PARTNER

In a paper titled "Physician Leadership in Changing Times," authors Jack Cochran, Gary Kaplan, and Rob Nesse, pose a critical question: *Who shall lead, and why?*

> The notion of joint or system wide accountability is gaining prominence, but which stakeholder—physicians, hospitals, health plans, or others—will lead delivery system transformation? *We believe it must be physicians* (emphasis added). Among

all providers, physicians have a disproportionate impact on the health care system, and therefore have a disproportionate opportunity and responsibility to lead change. Patients experience their own health and the health care system in many ways: physically, socially, psychologically, and financially. As the first and primary point of contact with the health care system for most patients, physicians must therefore act as caregivers, teachers, trusted information sources, and fiduciaries for their patients. They cannot and should not opt in and out of accountability toward their patients in any one of these roles.

This powerful statement serves as a redefinition of a physician's role—perhaps a broader definition than ever before. The authors insist that "physicians are ideally positioned, and in fact compelled, to take responsibility for helping shape the health care system—not just their own practice—to better serve patients' physical, social, psychological, and financial needs. That is a huge task, and it cannot be accomplished with passivity or indifference."

Some doctors will respond by saying that they already lead—they lead their office staff, their practice, their specialty, and so on. There are also many outstanding physician leaders at major medical centers, medical schools, professional societies, research institutes, and more—examples that demonstrate the potential of physician leadership. Yet throughout the profession an enormous amount of leadership potential remains untapped, and this cannot continue. Talented physician leaders must come off the sidelines and assert themselves more broadly, for never before has the health care industry so urgently needed vision and leadership. Historically, a wide variety of businesses have presented complex challenges to executive leaders, yet the enormity of the health care sector (nearly one-fifth of gross domestic product) and the staggering complexity of the business demand a level of leadership skill previously seen in only the best-led American companies.

Many doctors confuse *status* with leadership. This was a hallmark of a physician-centric world, but now that we are rapidly shifting to a patient-centric world, we recognize that status and leadership are often two entirely different dimensions.

In an ideal world, *all* physicians would be leaders with a clear commitment to patients in their journey through the health care system—caring about access, affordability, safety, *everything.* In this ideal state, physicians would eagerly take on broader responsibility, recognizing that with the unique influence doctors possess comes a responsibility for everything concerning a patient's health care experience. If the experience is found to be less than it should be, who better than the physician to lead the effort to set things right?

Healer

The fully accountable physician must fill the role of *healer-leader-partner.*

A physician as healer not only understands the need for strong clinical skills to be able to perform excellent medical or surgical care but also understands that the environment in which the patient and family exist is one of uncertainty and even fear. Physician as healer is a mind-set that should be understood and embraced, and in many ways physician as healer embodies aspects of the traditional definition of a good doctor.

Health professionals *chose* the occupation—it is our profession. All of us are here because we want to be here; we wanted to be doctors. But health care is very different for patients whose role is completely involuntary. No healthy adult or child dreams of some day becoming a patient. Nobody wakes up in the morning and says, "You know, I don't think I've ever been a patient. That sounds like something I might want to pursue." And nobody wakes up and says, "I haven't been a patient for a while. That sounds like something I need to go back to being." Being a patient is never, ever anything but involuntary. And, unfortunately, it is often all too instantaneous. Patients don't want to be sick, and they don't want to be in the medical system. All they want is to be healthy, but they often find themselves enmeshed in the health care system without a moment to prepare for it. They go from well to heart attack, from well to cancer diagnosis, from well to renal failure diagnosis, from well to trauma victim.

The healer role extends from the patient to her or his family and recognizes both the physical and emotional issues at stake. The healer acknowledges that great clinical care must always be patient-centered and that shared decision making with the patient is essential. In addition, the healer understands the concept of *nothing about me without me*.

The best healers have always been first and foremost patient-centered—it is always about the patient before it is about the system, the team, or anything else. Skilled healers are deeply knowledgeable about the best practices for the most common ailments, and they apply standard work—proven, reliable treatments—in such cases, knowing that it is safer and more reliable and that unwarranted variation means care that is not only suboptimal but also unnecessarily expensive. Healers also know that many of their patients do not fit easily into a best-practice category. These doctors are skilled at personalized, customized care for each individual patient who needs it—and this includes providers having the same level of empathy and support for all patients.

"Skilled healers—no matter their specialty—take care of the person, not the problem," observes Dr. Amy Compton-Phillips of Kaiser Permanente. "Orthopedic surgeons, for example, are not physicians for a body part. They are physicians for a person. This is complete care. It's when physicians across the spectrum take the position that a healer's role isn't to heal a *problem*, it is to heal a *person*."

Leader

As Cochran, Kaplan, and Nesse wrote, "We call on physicians as a profession to view leadership—and the development of leaders—as a key aspect of their role as advocate for their patients." A physician as leader acknowledges accountability for *all* of the elements that relate to a patient's experience, as defined by the Institute of Medicine's Six Aims. Physician as leader is in part about asking new questions—a shift from:

- How many patients can you *see* to how many patients' problems can you *solve*?
- How can we *encourage and convince* patients to get required prevention to how can we create pathways that significantly increase the likelihood that patients get required prevention, that make it easier for patients to be engaged in their health?
- *How often* should a physician see a patient in order to optimally monitor a condition to what is the *best*

way to optimally monitor a condition, taking into
account the context of that patient's life?

But let's not kid ourselves. The kind of physician leadership that we need in the United States is in short supply.
Too many physicians with great leadership potential opt
to sit on the sidelines. Paul O'Neill, former U.S. treasury
secretary and CEO of Alcoa, has worked intensively in
health care, and here's how he puts it: "The shortest skill
set in the world, including the United States, is the skill
set of real leaders. When I refer to 'real leaders,' I do
not include people who are appointed and designated
as leaders. We have a lot of them. Real leadership starts
from a proposition that you do not seek or accept a leadership designation because it pays better or because you
get more fame or recognition, but *because you hunger for
the responsibility of making a difference*" (emphasis added).

Gary Kaplan characterizes leadership as "a rare resource
in our industry. We have a tremendous opportunity to
define our *true north*. Being a professional means there is
something more important than our own self-interest. It's
about putting something higher, a higher calling. What
leaders do is change and elevate the conversation."

In the purest sense, all physicians ought to be leaders—someone who has a very clear commitment to
patients in their health care journey. This requires at a
minimum that *I am part of the solution. I am going to be
involved. I am going to opt in on problems that have an impact
on my patients.*

Patients have no better representative in the areas
that impact them than the clinician who serves them
and has been at their side. We have to stop looking at
the patient as a person with a clinical condition who

needs care today and instead view the patient as some-body who also has to be able to afford the care and have access to the care. We need to go from responsibility for the appointment or the operation to accountability for the broader patient experience. And we do not go to the sidelines when there is a significant issue—access, afford-ability, and much more—that requires leadership. We don't say, "Well, that one's not ours." We can't opt out. We have to opt in comprehensively on a broad range of issues that affect our patients.

Dr. Scott Young, coexecutive director of Kaiser Permanente's Care Management Institute, has a compelling take on the notion of a physician's broader responsibility to community and nation that echoes what Gary Kaplan said above. It is a privilege to be a doctor in our country, Young argues, and with that privilege come obligations. "Doctors do well economically and get a tremendous amount of recognition and respect," he says, "and as physicians we must always remember and appreciate that. The people in our community and our country are our responsibility."

Young contends that physicians in small-town practices where he came from in Oklahoma and in other small communities throughout the country understand this and are active in many different ways in their communities. They know their patients as neighbors and friends, as people they see in church, at youth sports, and in a variety of other activities.

But there is an empathy gap among some doctors. Recent research suggests that as young men and women progress through medical school and training, their sense of empathy diminishes. It is not that these idealistic young people do not care about their patients. They care very much. But as training progresses, doctors are inundated with information, and residents in particular are subjected to schedules that demand a grinding sense of survival. Yet when we go back and look at the personal statements that so many students wrote when applying to medical school, we find a depth of compassion and determination to heal and comfort the sick that is at the very foundation of health care in our country. Too often we drift from this. Medicine is a societal service to humanity. Doctors need to be present. Every time we opt out when a patient is having a problem, the patient loses a voice. We cannot sit on the sidelines.

It is important for young medical students and those in training to recognize their leadership responsibility and believe in themselves as professionals with strong leadership capabilities and potential. It is useful for some physicians to pursue more formal training and education, including obtaining an MBA, but we also need many more physicians who are willing and able to *lead from where they stand*. A growing cohort of physicians committed to leadership at many levels is critical for the transformation needed in health care. Effective leaders come in all shapes and sizes. No narrow classic prototype or stereotype of a leader exists. And the skills are not magical or mystical—most physicians are capable of learning them well.

Partner

Physician as partner means being a great team member and recognizes that the surest route to sustained quality care is through effective teamwork. An essential component of teamwork is not only how team members band together to care for the patient but also how team members treat one another. Physicians who have collegial professional relationships often get the most out of their teams. Partnering is about stepping up and addressing challenges that impact the ability of the team to care for patients; it is about identifying and eliminating barriers to excellent care. It is also about understanding information technology systems and making sure all team members are using the system effectively.

Physicians need to be central to the development of strong teams and to work with nurses, pharmacists, medical assistants, and others to ensure that they too have careers that are relevant, interesting, and satisfying. Some physicians condescend to nonphysician leaders from both hospitals and health plans. Yet a true physician partner—working closely with these leaders—can accomplish a great deal. Arrogance and condescension are toxic elements in a team setting.

This team-based approach demands the framework articulated by Paul O'Neill, who said that the best culture enables workers to "say yes to three questions every day: Am I treated with dignity and respect every day by everyone I encounter without regard to my gender, age, race, ethnicity, pay level, title, or any other qualifier? Am I given the things I need—education, training, encouragement, tools, financial resources—so that I can make a contribution to the organization that gives meaning to my life? And, am I recognized for what I do?"

This point of view is a profound statement of values, the kind of values that are powerful enough to help build a culture in which health care—or any other industry for that matter—can thrive.

We believe in this perspective because it is consistent with characteristics that physicians aspiring to the

healer-leader-partner role must possess. These characteristics include awareness, humility, and courage. Healer-
leader-partner physicians are constantly engaged with
the world of health care and are thus well aware of new
developments that can help them provide the best possible access and care for their patients. These doctors have
a sense of humility that enables them to recognize that
they cannot solve complex problems on their own but
must work in teams.

These physicians have the courage to act when doing
so benefits their patients. It takes courage for a physician
to drill down and examine the reality of the current state
in her or his practice. Courage is required, because when
the true current state is revealed—through value-stream
mapping or a similar technique—a bright light shines on
the massive amounts of waste in health care processes.
Increasingly, hospitals and physician practices are drawn
to *lean* management techniques whereby they map out
their services in terms of value for the patient. These value-stream maps reveal the truth; they reveal what benefits the patient and what might benefit the doctor or
hospital but not serve the patient. Facing the stark reality
of where value lies is often sobering as well as surprising
for physician leaders.

For example, when Dr. Bob Mecklenburg at Virginia
Mason in Seattle conducted a value-stream analysis of
treatment for uncomplicated low back pain, he and his
team discovered that virtually every step in the process
was waste and that only the application of physical therapy provided any real value to the patient. It took further
courage to lay this out with colleagues and customers—
as Mecklenburg did—and work jointly to eliminate the
waste and provide patients with value-added care and
only value-added care. And it takes humility as well to

set aside ego and long-standing tradition and face the true reality of the present state.

Healer-leader-partner physicians make it their business to study and understand the nature and impact of unwarranted variation in care throughout the nation and within individual physician practices or hospitals. Healer-leader-partner physicians think more broadly than is the tradition. They focus on the best medical solution to a patient's problem, but they also aspire to deliver the right care in the right setting at the right time for the right price. They think about and see the full continuum of care, and this includes identifying and eliminating unwarranted variation that is rampant throughout health care in the United States. This variation is so endemic to our system that it is found within very good provider organizations where doctors whose offices are across the hall from one another may very well solve a clinical problem in radically different ways, *with neither following evidence-based care guidelines*. Physicians have a responsibility to patients to seek out and apply evidence-based medicine when appropriate and to understand patients thoroughly so as to know when to modify or individualize care.

Healer-leader-partner physicians are committed to working with their patients in shared decision making, defined by the Center for Shared Decision Making at Dartmouth-Hitchcock Hospital as follows:

> Shared decision making is the collaboration between patients and caregivers to come to an agreement about a health care decision. It is especially useful when there is no clear "best" treatment option. The caregiver offers the patient information that will help him or her.

- Understand the likely outcomes of various options
- Think about what is personally important about the risks and benefits of each option
- Participate in decisions about medical care

When one overlays the reality of medical practice with the theory of physician as healer-leader-partner, a compelling picture emerges. We see practices where physicians aspire to this approach daily. Other practices are so siloed and stuck in the Industrial Age of care that there is nothing remotely resembling the healer-leader-partner mind-set.

The next few chapters tell a story that is both disturbing and uplifting. It is a story in which good people with noble aims crashed, a story in which a portion of a great organization seemed for a time to lose its way. It is, in fact, a story that teaches us profoundly important lessons for how we can find a far more efficient and productive pathway forward for physicians and their patients.

PART II
The Colorado Story

---

*Firsthand Lessons for Preserving
and Enhancing Physician Careers
to Provide Superb Patient Care*

In Part II, we shift gears. This is where I have an opportunity to reach back into my firsthand experience leading the Colorado Permanente Medical Group. No journey in health care follows a smooth pathway—the business is much too complex and unpredictable for that. Every day, health care organizations throughout the nation face a mind-boggling array of challenges, and that is just what we encountered in Colorado from the late 1990s into the 2000s. In many ways, the challenges in Colorado then were a microcosm of the challenges in health care across the United States today.

In the next four chapters I tell the story of a difficult period in Kaiser Permanente's history that serves as a lesson for our times, a story that defines the barriers we face in health care while simultaneously shining a bright light on solutions proven to work in the real world. This brief, aberrant slice of Kaiser Permanente's seventy-year history occurred during the 1990s at Kaiser Permanente Colorado. Having experienced firsthand this turbulent period, I am convinced that it contains valuable lessons for the challenges prevalent throughout health care today.

Jack Cochran, MD

4

Evolution of a Physician Leader

I'm not sure we're going to survive with a soul.

BREAKING THE SPIRIT OF THE PLACE

The problems at Kaiser Permanente (KP) in Colorado in the 1990s constituted a kind of perfect storm: patient, staff, and physician satisfaction rates sharply declined, while the physician turnover rate accelerated. In just two years KP Colorado lost twelve thousand members and faced a series of financial challenges.

Within this Colorado storm swirled a variety of forces: cynicism, leadership issues, poor communication among leaders and physicians, and even a lack of trust in physicians as partners in the enterprise. The people involved in all stages of the Colorado effort—even when things were going sideways—were never doing anything other than what they believed at the time was in the best interest of patients. But this is a story of change, and change is rarely easy. Jobs were lost, egos were bruised, and dedicated people made decisions that impeded progress.

In the mid-1990s, before I was involved in leadership, the KP Colorado team brought in a prominent consultancy to help guide us out of the mess. Not at all unreasonably, our leaders at the time had confidence in the consultants' analysis and prescription—and with good reason. The consulting firm possessed an excellent track record, and the consultants' analysis was in fact pretty well on the mark: KP Colorado had problems with access, service, and more.

All of us who practice medicine know that administrative challenges can be a major hindrance to our ability to provide high-quality, efficient care. Challenges such as too much paperwork—a euphemism for too much nondoctor work—were (and often still are) ubiquitous throughout health care. Provider organizations throughout the country struggled to find solutions. The consulting team made three main recommendations that were designed to get the region back on track. They first suggested setting up a hospitalist service whereby physicians with particular expertise in hospital-based care delivery focused on in-patients, as opposed to using a traditional clinic-based practice. While this initially drew significant criticism, over time the hospitalist program proved to be quite successful.

The consultants also recommended that KP Colorado set up a centralized call center. They saw no reason to have a variety of KP locations in Colorado answering phones and making appointments. Instead, the consultants recommended a centralized facility where in theory the operator would quickly shift the patient to a nurse line or find an open appointment slot. The idea was that a centralized call operation would make it easier for patients to schedule appointments and would ease the administrative burden on clinics.

This required shifting nurses out of clinics and into the call center to field patient calls. Thus, the first two changes recommended by consultants and implemented by the leadership team were both immediately disruptive to physicians' practice routines.

The third change—customer-directed access—exacerbated the problems. The notion was that each patient should link to a health care team that included a couple of primary care doctors, several nurses, and other clinical support team members. Again, on the surface this sounded sensible enough. But the reality was that this approach solved the access problem but did so at the expense of continuity of care—a high price to pay. Customer-directed access was essentially an idea that was intended to give patients what they said they wanted—appointments as soon as possible. "You want to come in? We'll get you in! But in with whom?" Patients got appointments more quickly but too often *not* with their doctors—which was immensely frustrating to both patients and physicians.

Here is how my physician colleague Dr. Bill Marsh put it: "If you are a doctor, your world has been disrupted in a major way. You are not following your own patients in the hospital any longer—a hospitalist is doing that—and there's an appointment jam-up and you have fewer RNs [registered nurses] to work with you in the clinic. When the changes happened, we broke continuity with the primary care doctors."

Instead of seeing their own doctor nearly 70 percent of the time, patients saw their doctor about 30 percent of the time. Far too often there were situations in clinics where doctors across the hall from one another were *seeing one another's patients on the same day!*

Another physician colleague, Bill Wright, then chief of primary care, was acutely aware of the pressures on all of the primary care doctors. But he also believed that the problems within the medical group constituted what he termed "self-inflicted wounds." Says Wright, "Seeing another physician's patient while my colleague across the hall was seeing my patient was ridiculous."

Not only did this disrupt important and long-standing physician-patient relationships—and arguably caused the quality of care to suffer—but it also had debilitating financial consequences. There is a huge difference between seeing a patient I know well—whose conditions I have been treating for years—and seeing a patient for the first time. In the latter case, when a physician is in doubt he or she may well be more likely to run additional tests, send a patient to the Emergency Department, or even admit the patient. Thus, KP Colorado was experiencing service and continuity issues but was also adding to the cost of care. The result was increased Emergency Department costs of an additional 25–30 percent per year.

Bill Marsh summarized it well. "When you break continuity with the patients, the doctors are less familiar with a patient. Continuity matters in health care."

Frontline physicians pushed back. Yet the leadership—ironically most of whom were physicians—seemed to convey a belief that we doctors were difficult and needed to be managed, *that we were part of the problem.* Changes were done *to* doctors rather than *with* doctors. Unfortunately, the leaders were not listening to frontline physicians. The problem was both operational and attitudinal and created an environment that many felt was demeaning to physicians. Over time, many of us came to believe that the core issue was the exclusion of doctors from the decision-making process. Discontent was rampant throughout the medical group. Bill Marsh became so fed up with the way things were going that he did something that had never been done in the Colorado Permanente Medical Group (CPMG): he called an all-hands meeting that attracted two hundred to three hundred physicians. According to Marsh, "My thinking for calling the meeting was that there were serious credibility issues with leadership, and although I was a new associate medical director, we had to start somewhere to regain trust, and the place to start was to simply and honestly say we have screwed things up and we must make course corrections." He stood up in front of the medical group and apologized "for the mess that had been created."

Larry Hergott, a cardiologist, had been with KP for many years. A great gentleman, he was one of those doctors who quietly went about his business delivering superb care and developing excellent relationships with his patients. In the months before the election for seats on the CPMG Board of Directors, a dozen or so candidates presented their case for why they should be elected. There were face-to-face meetings and discussions and question-and-answer periods—a sort of minicampaign. Everyone running that night had declared their candidacy many weeks if not months earlier.

During that time, Hergott looked around and did not like what he saw. He was deeply proud of the KP care delivery model, but he could clearly see that something had gone wrong. And he'd had enough.

The night of the election, Hergott declared himself a candidate. He rose to speak, and as he did so a hush fell over the room. He spoke of his love for the practice and for the special way that KP delivered patient-centered, evidence-based, compassionate health care for more than three decades. He said that he thought things were off track—that there was a kind of mean-spiritedness in the air.

"You know," he said, "I think that Kaiser Permanente will survive. It will find ways to keep the business running. But I want to be on the board because I'm not sure we're going to survive with a soul."

Hergott's election-night speech to the physician group was earnest and memorable, but it was more than that. Here was a physician with courage and commitment standing up as a leader. It was a testimony to the power of physician leaders at all levels. There was a critical object lesson here: that physician leadership need not come only from those with titles. Leadership must come from physicians *wherever they are,* using their commitment to patients to guide and lead organizations toward a better and more patient-centered approach to care.

RADICAL CONCEPT: "I WOULD JUST LIKE TO HAVE MORE BALANCED CONVERSATIONS"

I never thought of myself as someone who would run for office within the medical group, but during this turbulent period colleagues who had worked with me through the years suggested that I run. And when I asked why, they told me that I had been a reliable partner through the years. One colleague said he knew that if they needed me to come in to operate on a patient with a dog bite at 3:00 a.m., I showed up; I didn't try to talk the team out of the urgency of the situation. I had always prided myself on my determination to be the best surgeon I could possibly be, but I learned in this stressful time that my friends and colleagues also considered me a good listener.

When I looked around at the challenges at KP Colorado, it struck me that my colleagues were angry and disenchanted because a bureaucracy was preventing them from fulfilling their mission to provide high-quality, affordable health care to our members. Colleagues I had known for years urged me to run for the board, and many could not conceal their anger about the existing conditions within the medical group. "You have to do it, Jack. There's so much chaos. It's a mess."

For me, the canary in the coal mine was seeing top-notch primary care doctors leave. It was alarming and spoke volumes about the dysfunction at the time. During just a two-year period, 20 percent of our primary care doctors left the practice.

When I ran for the board in 1996, my platform was simple: I wanted to listen to physicians. I wanted to understand the very real business challenges facing our group. I wanted to have *thoughtful, balanced conversations about what was going on*. When the votes were counted, I had won a seat on the board. A year later I was elected chair.

During my two years of serving on the board there were some incremental changes in policies at the medical group, yet culturally little had changed. In fact, anger and resentment among the physicians continued to define the organization.

This persistent fever of disaffection among doctors drove a number of them to urge me to run for executive medical director (in effect, CEO of the CPMG). But I said the same thing to each of them: "I don't have a portfolio or extensive experience running a business. I barely balance my own checkbook."

The turning point came in November 1998, when Bill Marsh and I were among a small number of KP leaders selected to attend an advanced leadership program at the

University of North Carolina. The first night there, Bill sat down and spoke privately with me.

"I want you to run for medical director," Bill said.

"Against *you*?"

"No," Bill said. "I want you to run, and I want to work for you. As board chair, you've come in and brought sanity to the conversations. You're not a fire brand. But you force us to move in directions where we have to confront reality."

Bill said that it was time to create a powerful movement to do nothing less than fundamentally alter the culture of CPMG, and I was deeply affected by this. Back in Denver, a number of other physicians similarly urged me to run, including Dr. Berry Morton, who told me, "It's your time, it's your turn, we need you."

There were about a dozen applicants for the executive medical director position, and each candidate was subjected to a preliminary interview with the board, after which the field of possibilities would be cut in half. My effort got off to an inauspicious start. After the first round of interviews, Larry Hergott approached me and said, "You were really unimpressive, Jack, really flat. You had no enthusiasm, no passion. Do you want this job or not, Jack? Because if you don't make the cut, you're going to regret it forever."

I was shaken by his comments. My sometimes laid-back style had made me appear in the board meeting as though I was a reluctant candidate. But I was not reluctant! I knew by this point that I badly wanted the job; I wanted it because I believed that I could do it.

While my baseline approach was to have balanced conversations, the reality was that the message had greater depth and power than that. As my platform emerged over time, it was clear that physicians must step up and solve the health care crisis. We must be part of the solution—we must be creative and bold and stand up for our patients.

This was the right prescription at the right time. In November 1998, the board voted 7 to 1 to elect me their leader. When the matter was put to the physicians to affirm the board vote, the tally was 342 to 2.

I just listened. . . . They were very unhappy and angry.

I was elected executive medical director in November 1998 but would not assume the leadership role until January 2000. This was fortunate. I knew that I needed time to prepare for a job that was about as radically different from my twenty-plus years in the operating room as I could imagine.

Although I had certainly not drawn a detailed blueprint, I did have an approach. Two priorities topped my list: I wanted to talk face-to-face with as many of the five hundred KP Colorado doctors as possible, and I wanted to learn as much as I could about leadership and business, which included attending a Stanford University executive leadership program.

Sometimes the most important step that leaders can take is to recognize what they do *not* know. I was very clear when elected that I did not have extensive business experience. I knew that I would have to work doubly hard to understand how to lead effectively in a complex environment. I needed to learn not only what to change but also—and more important—how to *lead* change. To do so, I would have to listen and learn.

I hit the road in March 1999 for what I called my Listening Tour. I felt a powerful impulse to get out there and listen to what the doctors had to say. I needed to look them in the eye and feel their frustration; I needed to hear about and understand what they were experiencing. I also sought to send a signal that I cared deeply about what the physicians thought and felt.

I could have met with a representative sampling of physicians, but I wanted to hear *everybody*. In this sense, the Listening Tour served as an act of respect for my physician colleagues and an opportunity for me to be as well grounded in their reality as possible. I was very open with doctors that I did not have a specific plan for how to run the place but that I would build such a plan based on what I heard from them, which is precisely what I did.

From March until mid-June 1999, when I would start the Stanford program, I put a few thousand miles on my car visiting doctors. I carried with me nothing but a pad of paper and a pen. I went out to the clinics one after another, typically spending the better part of a day at each one. In advance I would schedule fifty-minute meetings each hour with four to five physicians—thirty to forty doctors per day. I would spend more than 90 percent of each session listening and taking notes. I heard about frustration with the call center, confusion about scheduling, and irritation at not having the full teams needed to deliver high-quality patient care. I heard and felt frustration with and anger at the group leadership. The messages from each physician at each clinic seemed to be dispiriting echoes of one another.

I did not offer solutions to the problems that the physicians raised. I did not commiserate with *"yeah, everything sucks."* I just listened. And what I heard at clinic after clinic, from physician after physician, was that they were deeply unhappy and often angry.

At one clinic in particular, I found that the staff was not angry so much as they were infused with a sense of futility. It was as though they were at a dead end and there was nothing they could do.

During the Listening Tour, I learned a critical lesson: the difference between cynicism and dissent. Cynics are characterized by a sense of hopelessness and futility and do not present alternative solutions along with their criticism. A *dissenter*, however, wanted to work to make the organization more effective. Thus, I learned a valuable lesson: Dissent has value, while cynicism has none.

Dissent can be just as angry as cynicism but comes with engagement: *I care enough to be angry about the situation here.* Dissent comes with ideas for change and solutions for improvement. Dissent is forward thinking and solution oriented. Cynicism is futile, hopeless, and negative.

Challenging futility is an essential component of leadership. Futility doesn't help me. Can you take that and turn it into a request, a proposal for change, an idea? In a sense, *all leadership is change leadership.* This requires real understanding of the point of view of those who will be affected by whatever the change might be. Here is where the Listening Tour played an essential role.

Instinctively and through experience, I understood that change was not dictatorial in nature but instead was more subtle, more personal. Change required listening and understanding. I had long ago learned to listen actively, that is, to listen to what the person was trying to convey to me. Too often I had seen people pretend to listen, but their version of listening was little more than a break between pronouncements. They appeared to listen while forming the next thought that they would articulate.

I had been drawn to an idea articulated by Randall Root, founder of Root Publishing and a respected thinker concerning strategic engagement work with employees. Root's notion was that when taking on challenging problems, it was essential that both parties share all their data. *If I have your data and you have mine, we can get somewhere.* Valuing dissent is saying, *I don't agree with you, but I am working with you. With my data and yours, we'll meet and find a solution.*

THE SURGICAL SPECIALISTS'
UGLY CONFLICT

If there was a situation within KP Colorado that embodied the turbulence of the times and represented the epitome of cynicism, it was a surgical specialty department's conflict. Certainly it was among the most extreme manifestations of the culture, yet the fact that the conflict had festered over a period of years conveyed a sense of how unfortunately out of balance the medical group culture had become. It was a harsh lesson that sometimes—even with talented physicians—a Hollywood ending remains illusory.

In the autumn of 1999 before I had even taken over as leader of the medical group, I was drawn into this rancorous internal conflict between competing teams of surgical specialists. This was the sort of ego-driven conflict that can happen when extremely smart people accustomed to having their way vehemently disagree with equally smart people accustomed to having their way. Patients rarely see it, but leaders within health care organizations throughout the country deal with it every day. In this particular case, the board—immensely frustrated by the situation—had tried a variety of moves to placate and manage the two opposing teams, even going so far as to place a physician from a different specialty in charge of the group (Dr. Bill Marsh, pediatric pulmonologist).

Why do these sorts of stories matter? They matter because they are the antithesis of physician as healer-leader-partner. They embody cynicism rather than a constructive dose of dissent. Cynicism is antithetical to teamwork and to respecting and supporting one's colleagues and is anything but patient-centered. Ultimately, there is something both infuriating and sad when competent professionals engage in this sort of conflict.

And to say the least, the timing was unfortunate. I had completed my Listening Tour and come away with a strong emotional connection to all of the physicians who felt trapped in a dysfunctional system. The Listening Tour had been one of the most powerfully defining experiences of my career. I ached for these colleagues and wanted to do whatever it took to make things right so that we could provide the finest possible care for our patients. After the Listening Tour, I had limited patience for the ego-fueled sideshow that was this surgical department's conflict.

Eight surgical specialists, four against four, went to the mat against one another because of individual personalities. There were personal differences of philosophy, style, and clinical approaches. Even with that, all eight doctors provided superb care to their patients. But their dislike for one another made any semblance of harmony impossible.

With three hundred thousand patients to care for, I found this level of internal animosity unprofessional and completely unacceptable. Leaders had worked to solve the problem by separating the groups on two different floors and hiring a professional facilitator to work with the entire group for more than a year. But the recalcitrance on the part of the two factions was unusually fierce.

At a regular board meeting, Team A entered and made its case that the future needed to look different. The team members were trying to do some innovative things, but Team B wouldn't let it happen. Team A's solution, and its request, was that we fire Team B. Then Team B presented its position to the board and accused Team A of failing to deliver quality care. Not only that, but Team B also said that its members could handle more volume than Team A.

After this, a physician colleague asked me what I was going to do. I said, "I don't have any idea what to do. For one thing, I'm never going to meet with them in separate groups again. If we're going to meet with them, we're going to meet with them together." I insisted on this because separate sessions only served to strengthen their divisiveness. The idea that we accommodated their apartness—their unwillingness to work together as a single team—bothered me greatly. Yet in such an intensely emotional environment, the solution was not readily clear.

My colleague set up a meeting for the two of us to meet with all eight surgeons together. He phoned me the afternoon of the meeting and said, "So what are you going to say tonight?" And I said, "I honestly don't know. I really don't know what to say to these guys. They have had two years of facilitation and counseling. They had an external consultant come in for two years who tried to get them to work together. I don't know what to say to them."

I next met my physician colleague in the parking garage before the meeting, and he asked, "Well, do you know what you're going to say yet?"

I said, "I actually don't. I have no solution."

He said, "Well, this is great. We're about to walk in there."

I said, "I know, I know. I'll do some listening."

I could tell what he was thinking: *Great, you're really decisive!*

We arrived at the meeting, and there they were. Four of the surgeons sat on one side, and the other four sat on the other side. They were all glum and serious. They all thought that they had the inside track to getting the other team fired. Each faction firmly believed that it held the moral high ground. And the thing that's interesting is that underlying the tension, it was a superior clinical department. They were all really damn good clinicians and surgeons.

My colleague said, "We'd like to thank you guys for coming here tonight. Jack and I have given this a lot of thought, and we're really enthused about working with you now."

I'm watching these guys, and they were not listening to anything. They just sat there glaring. My physician colleague said, "I will commit to you that whatever the board needs to do to work this out, we will do it. And I think Jack's very interested in making this an early improvement in his administration. What do you think, Jack?"

I said, "I must say, this is a new one for me. I've never seen this kind of civil war behavior before. And I know all of you, and I've worked with all of you, and I've operated with most of you. And I would send my family to any of you. But I think you guys have actually given this your best thinking, and I think you have actually come to us with a solution. And you all believe it's the solution, and so I believe it's the solution. And the solution is to start firing members of your department. So, I'm going to ask the board to put together a grid of the eight of you, and we're going to consider a dismissal plan. But if the first dismissal comes from Team A, the second one comes from Team B. And then the third one comes from Team A, and the fourth one comes from Team B. And we will continue until we get a nucleus of people who want to work together."

And I walked out. Enough was enough. This problem had been tolerated for too long.

A minute later my colleague came out after me and asked, "Are you going back in there?"

I said, "No. They gave us their best thinking. Get the grid. Let's put out a grid and develop a plan."

He said, "Go back in there. What the hell are you doing? We've only been in there for ten minutes."

I said, "I'm done. They brought me their best thinking. I processed it. I gave it back to them. The only thing I didn't give back to them was whether Team A or B was first. We're going to eliminate individuals from alternating teams until we get back to a viable entity."

He said, "Good Lord, you are going to be a problem."

I asked, "Do you have a better solution?"

He says, "No, but I didn't expect you to say that."

So, I went back and I told the board, "I want you guys to get the best metrics you can on the eight physicians. All eight of them have come to us with a solution that we need to fire doctors. That will be our plan."

Board members were shocked. Some were apoplectic. Nothing like this had ever happened before—not on this scale. Board members said that everybody's going to call. You guys are going to start firing doctors.

I said, "Well, we're not going to fire anybody who is doing productive work and is a good citizen. But we have to have people who are good citizens. This is a group practice. It has to have that kind of ethic. It's their solution. We're just going to accept it."

And over the period of a year, one of the two groups left on their own. I think the lesson is that you can't let something fester forever. And this had been festering for two years. We had done counseling. We had tried facilitation. We had separated them. And then they came to the board and insisted that the solution was firing colleagues. And what I finally decided was that they were right. They had painted themselves and the medical group into a corner. It was really a shame, because these doctors had a strong reputation in the community, but they autoimploded. So we hired new doctors, and the department has become strong and collaborative.

5

Jack's Constants

Preservation and Enhancement of Career

The place was psychologically on fire.

Was I ready to lead a business of this size and complexity? The answer, by any traditional definition, was no. But I believed that listening to my physician colleagues would initiate a direction and a focus forward—and that is precisely what happened.

I believed that physicians could and should be leaders and that with physician leaders marbled throughout the organization, great things were possible. I believed that effective leaders come in all shapes and sizes. While my experience as a surgeon with a modest amount of leadership experience was hardly ideal preparation, I did feel that there were only a few basic characteristics required to learn how to become a leader. Listening effectively and understanding were big ones. A sense of humility was important as well, especially given the daunting nature of the task ahead. In this period of instability, we needed thoughtful, balanced conversations and a steady leadership team.

If you looked under the hood of the Kaiser Permanente (KP) Colorado operation during the period when my leadership team and I were working on the turnaround, you would find an interesting mix of parts. And one of the more important parts was a team with a genuine sense of humility. I would tell my team, "I don't know the answers. I did not come to you with a prefabricated solution. But I think I know what questions to ask, and I listen carefully."

And with humility comes a genuine desire—a need, actually—to learn. And that's what my mission had been before taking over the medical group: to learn as much as I could. I read a great deal and was particularly impacted by Jim Collins's book *Good to Great: Why Some Companies Make the Leap . . . and Others Don't.* As much as any other book of its kind, this one deeply affected me. I have reread it a number of times, and it has helped me learn how to lead; it has helped me clarify the tone and point of view of my leadership. I aspired to achieve what Collins characterized as "Level 5 leadership"—the highest level. Collins defined Level 5 as a leader who "builds enduring greatness through a paradoxical combination of personal humility plus professional will."

From experience, reading, and observation, I could see that many leaders were arrogant or heroic and were motivated by self-promotion. I believed that listening well was an act of sincerity, because real listening means that you are eager to learn. For me, the Listening Tour was not a public relations initiative but instead was an effort to make clear that I did not have all of the answers I needed to run the organization but knew that I could find those answers from frontline physicians. I adopted the Level 5 notion of learning from colleagues and their teams.

The Listening Tour had been akin to a graduate-level course in the reality of the clinical front lines. That summer of 1999, I enrolled in the seven-week Stanford Business School Executive Program. I was something of an anomaly in the class of about fifty students, most of whom were successful businesspeople preparing to take over C-suite positions and had come to Stanford for a refresher.

For me, though, it was quite different. I was intimidated by the immersion into business courses—I had never taken one in my life. And I found myself at the bottom of the ladder and feeling somewhat overwhelmed.

Fortunately, I quickly found a professor whose message had deep resonance for me. Jeffrey Pfeffer, Stanford Business School professor of organizational behavior, was an easygoing man about my age who held a rock-solid belief—based on years of rigorous academic analysis— that the key to success in business was *treating people well*. I loved this idea! And I was captivated by Pfeffer's book *The Human Equation: Building Profits by Putting People First*. As I read the book, it was as though Pfeffer was reinforcing and providing an evidence base for every instinct I had about how I would lead the KP Colorado region. As the description for Pfeffer's book put it, "Why is common sense so uncommon when it comes to managing people? How is it that so many seemingly intelligent organizations implement harmful management practices and ideas?"

According to Pfeffer, "A lot of organizations want change, but they don't want to do anything differently. They don't have intent or clarity of purpose. They tend to benchmark their organizations against what everybody else is doing, and so they do what everyone else does. Everybody wants great results, but they do it by doing what everybody else is doing—because it feels safe." Pfeffer has dealt with many Fortune 500 corporations and has often found that senior leaders lack clarity of focus on what actually matters. "Most people spend their time on fifty things, two of which actually matter," he says.

After the Stanford course, discussions with Pfeffer, the Listening Tour, and hours of quiet reflection, I arrived at a crucial realization: the turnaround of KP Colorado depended on human resources but a kind of human resources that would be radically different from what had been the norm at KP Colorado. This would be human resources framed by a set of values centered on treating professionals well, demanding a great deal from them, measuring them, counseling them when necessary, and disciplining or even dismissing them when appropriate—but always working toward a collegial, respectful culture that honored the medical profession.

I convened the first meeting of the leadership team—seven physicians—in early 1999. I asked everybody to write down the elements of what their role would be, and we had a useful discussion that naturally led to the priorities that, for me, were the essence of our mission. (These came to be known throughout the organization as "Jack's Constants.") My constants were simple:

- Preservation and enhancement of career,
- Optimizing the patient care experience, and
- Streamlining the care process.

PRESERVATION AND ENHANCEMENT OF CAREER

The bedrock element was preservation and enhancement of career. Without it, success on the other two constants was impossible. I found the organization psychologically on fire. People were hurting. I was determined to bring back reverence for the career of all the caregivers, starting with physicians. My belief was that in a culture of professionals, you live or die based on their morale, enthusiasm, and commitment.

I told the team that I wanted to find out "what happened to the idealist—that nineteen-year-old who dreamed of becoming a doctor." It was an important insight into the real problem underlying all the other problems at KP Colorado and beyond. It was the notion that there had been a kind of unintended bait and switch in medicine, that extremely bright young men and women had gone into medicine with a powerful motivation to heal the sick, and they did so expecting a certain type of experience and life and had found—many to their deep and even angry dismay—that the rules had changed. Instead of autonomy, doctors felt bound to an assembly line. Instead of authority, they were pleading with insurance bureaucracies to get tests, procedures, and medications for their patients.

What had gone wrong at KP Colorado was complicated, because I knew that in the vast majority of KP locations the physician experience was deeply rewarding. KP has always been different from most other provider organizations. KP's integrated nature enables doctors to do what is best for patients without undue interference from insurance companies, which is a source of terrible strain for millions of other physicians nationwide.

But at KP Colorado we had gotten off track. I saw firsthand that the passion and idealism of these young doctors had been bled out of them by a sadly dysfunctional health care system. It was puzzling to me because I still had a deep appreciation for my career and loved being a doctor, and I wanted to try to understand what it would take to rekindle the passion in as many of my colleagues as possible. Being a physician comes with the profound responsibility of caring for people when they are at their most vulnerable. I consider it the greatest professional honor possible.

I knew that no significant change in care delivery, culture, or anything else was remotely possible without physician support. And this meant doing things that enhanced physicians careers, recognized the importance of their roles, and provided the full support they needed to deliver great care.

As a physician for three decades, I knew that the only way to rally the support of other physicians was with honest, direct discussion. You cannot fool, manipulate, or bully doctors. Any attempt to do so will fail. You must engage them in an honest fashion.

The systems that had been established to support physician practices were inadequate and prevented doctors from performing at peak capacity. Staff support and systems were so ineffective that it was impossible to get enough productivity out of a potentially highly productive physician.

Bill Marsh says that the impact of the first constant was almost immediate and very powerful. "To hear the leader of the medical group talk about preservation and enhancement of career—to know that it was even on the radar screen—was a breath of fresh air. *Someone in leadership understands how hard we are trying and honors what we do. Oh my god!* The medical group is the heart and soul of KP, and you needed their hearts and souls, not just their presence, and that's what Jack went after."

While preservation and enhancement of career would be the bedrock of the new culture, it was not without some controversy. Wasn't medicine all about being patient-centered? How could the first constant involve doctors and not patients?

Dr. Bill Wright, who served as the leader in primary care, argued that preservation and enhancement of career might send the wrong message to some people. "Preservation and enhancement of career *so that what?* So that you can do patient-centered care? And while most doctors intuitively got it, some didn't." Wright thought that there was enough uncertainty or ambiguity in that first constant so that it should have been explicitly altered with a clear enunciation of the goal: *to be patient-centered.*

The structure at KP aligns a medical group leader— my role—with a partner on the health plan side. Typically, throughout the KP system these partnerships are quite effective. The idea is that within the integrated organization, the partners work side by side for the benefit of the organization overall. But when I went to my counterpart, I ran into some turbulence. After I explained my three constants, my colleague replied, "Boy, you really don't know what's going on, do you? We're losing money. We're losing members. And you're promising you're going to protect the doctors."

She was certainly motivated to improve the organization, but her solution was to withhold a certain percentage of physician compensation, which doctors would then be able to earn back based on performance. This approach had worked in some organizations, yet after the Listening Tour it was the polar opposite of the signal I wanted to send regarding preservation and enhancement of career.

From my perspective, preservation and enhancement of career *never meant* protection at any cost. Over and over again I repeated a sort of mantra: *physician as leader, not victim, never tyrant.*

I told my health plan partner that if we don't make physician careers something that they want to remain in, we will never be successful. She pushed back, insisting that more financial incentives for doctors were essential, but I vetoed the idea. I believed that taking compensation away from physicians to start with was exactly the wrong message. Financial incentives can be appropriate for physicians in some instances, but given the challenges at KP Colorado, this was not one of those times.

More than that, I recognized the compelling case that Dr. Eric Christiansen made for increasing compensation for primary care physicians. Christiansen, who later became chief of family medicine, was a persistent advocate for recognizing that primary care physicians were underpaid. He had received little attention from leadership. Christiansen and I explored a variety of options to improve primary care compensation. It was complex and by no means easy, but working together we got it done, and it proved to be a crucial proof point of my preservation and enhancement constant. Getting this accomplished had significant value. It boosted morale for primary care doctors and gave our new leadership team serious credibility for our ability to get things done.

This one particular move not only provided primary care physicians with a more appropriate level of compensation but also measurably raised their job-satisfaction scores and helped to energize the primary care practice. It was not that the primary care doctors were looking for the keys to the kingdom. But when physicians feel as though they are not getting a fair deal financially, this strikes directly at morale. Money is surely not the driver for the vast majority of doctors, but when physicians feel unfairly compensated, it creates a nagging sense of dissatisfaction that needs to be addressed. Once addressed, doctors' sense of satisfaction is derived much more from a sense of mission to care for their patients. From the start I had a sense of great confidence that working closely with an excellent board of directors, we would somehow get it right and could fix the place. I believed this because I knew that there was a certain ethos within the DNA of KP. There had always been a deeply rooted sense of integrity within KP. Our values as an organization were so clearly focused on caring for our patients—and always had been—that it gave me a sense of confidence that if my leadership team and I worked in sync with the board and if we made decisions informed by the traditions of KP's integrity and values, we would be successful.

OPTIMIZING THE PATIENT CARE EXPERIENCE

The second constant, optimizing the care experience, focused on improving service and quality for our members—phone service, primary care access, and much more. A central part of optimizing the care experience involved the use of technology to manage populations of patients with chronic conditions.

Dr. John Merenich led this work with great insight and intensity. Merenich started his work focusing on the more than fifteen thousand patients with cardiovascular disease who had experienced a previous heart attack and were thus at much higher risk for a subsequent event. But when managed properly, these patients could thrive. Merenich built a registry of all the patients in this category and worked closely with cardiologists and primary care teams to identify best practices for maintaining the health of these patients.

"The big breakthrough," says Merenich, "was bringing in the clinical pharmacy specialists as a new members of the team. The doctors wanted to track everything, but the clinical pharmacists were well trained for this work and got great results. This freed the physicians to focus on more complex cases."

The program had been in place for just two years when it rocketed KP Colorado to the top of the national standings, landing in the number-one slot on the National Commission on Quality Assurance's HEDIS (Healthcare Effectiveness Data and Information Set) measure, which is used by health plans to measure performance on dozens of quality metrics. A critical component to the success was that Merenich treated all team members—no matter their position—as equals. Merenich's respect lifted the teams morale. His view for all the team members was "you are my brother; you are my sister." This inspired the clinical pharmacists and propelled the KP Colorado clinical pharmacy program to new heights. Based on HEDIS measures, KP Colorado went from the top quartile in 1998 to the top decile and into the top ten, all the way to number one, by 2007. Dr. Andy Lum deserved huge credit for much of our service-improvement work. Andy's patient-focused leadership provided positive reinforcement to our clinicians. His infectious optimism helped lead important changes within our organization.

STREAMLINING THE CARE PROCESS

Streamlining the care process—the third constant— meant taking on the behemoth that is waste in health care. Various estimates from the Institute of Medicine and others suggest that as much as 30 percent of the money spent on health care is wasted. The new leadership team sought to "eliminate waste in all the right ways," says Dr. Patty Fahy, a member of my core team who played a pivotal role as head of Human Resources.

One powerful example of streamlining the care process came about by happenstance. When the idea to shift nurses out of clinics and put them on phone lines took place, most physicians were upset with the loss of their nurses. Clinics failed to function well with primary care teams that were badly strained.

Then a nurses' strike forced the medical group to put doctors on the phone lines to handle the many questions from patients. Nurses had performed very well in this role, but in certain instances doctors were able to make a rapid diagnosis over the phone, thus reducing the use of the Emergency Department and cutting the hospital admission rate. As a result, nurses returned to the clinics where they were needed and performed at a very high level, and doctors remained on the phones. One benefit of having nurses freed from phone duty was that they were strong partners in every clinic and were key to working with patients on a variety of issues, including complex patients with multiple chronic conditions. (In recent years throughout KP, the nurse advice line has been an excellent source of information and advice for millions of patients.)

A second example involved in streamlining the care process was in plastic surgery. Instead of requiring patients to come into the clinic, get checked, and then come back for minor surgery, a whole step was removed. According to Bill Marsh,

The way it used to work was a member would come in and meet a plastic surgeon for a consult, the surgeon would then schedule surgery for treatment of a skin cancer. Then Berry Morton, one of the plastic surgeons, and Carrie Newman, project manager with surgical specialties, had a new idea. If the primary care physician or dermatologist confirmed the lesion was a basal cell cancer, why not just directly schedule the patient for removal in the minor procedure room? When we measured patient satisfaction, the patients loved it, the surgeons loved it, and we eliminated one unnecessary visit to the surgeon that could be used for other more serious patients.

With open clinic appointments, our time to surgery went from eighty days to fourteen days, resulted in improved quality, patient-centeredness, and staff satisfaction.

Other changes were stickier, particularly in primary care where the situation was so challenging. Primary care physicians were faced with ever-expanding workloads—prevention, screening, and monitoring patients with multiple chronic conditions—that required additional time. By listening to the doctors, we made significant changes to improve the working conditions for primary care physicians and enable them to provide better care for their patients. First, we began to slowly lower panel size—the number of patients assigned to each physician. This made the lives of physicians much more reasonable and allowed them to give more attention to patients. Adding more nurses and physician assistants strengthened the primary care teams. And clinic hours were shortened (during times of light patient traffic), yet with doctors working with their teams and by using smaller panel sizes, they were able to solve more patient problems in a day than when the clinic hours were longer. The key was to make sure that everyone on the team worked at the top of their license and that tasks that could be done by other team members were handled by them, thereby freeing the doctor to focus on complex, nuanced cases.

The challenge was not just clinical. It was a multipart business turnaround, a need to simultaneously improve morale, patient service, and finances. Our team members took on a variety of jobs, including stabilizing the medical groups' finances and tightening information technology to clear away clutter and provide physicians with an intuitive electronic system.

At the same time, human resources leader Patty Fahy created a comprehensive human resources strategy. Fahy's work was essential to building an invigorated new culture. This challenge is never easy in any company or industry, and it may well be that it is particularly difficult in a health care environment, especially a troubled one. Essentially, Fahy's assignment was to hire and retain great people and support them with the systems and procedures that made it increasingly possible for them to provide excellent patient care.

The attitude and approach toward doctors shifted rapidly when my team and I took over leadership of the medical group. Programs were transformed: physician orientation, leadership training, and communication approaches were created or revamped. We went from limiting information about the practice and its challenges to making the business transparent, from generally excluding doctors to including them in everything—soliciting their views and participation in every area of the business from what insurance products to offer in the marketplace to exactly how those products would be packaged.

Says Fahy, "Physician as leader was such a core concept for me. I interviewed leaders on the board, the health plan leadership team, and on our CPMG [Colorado Permanente Medical Group] leadership team regarding what would be the best traits of physician as leader. This was not referring to physicians in formal leadership roles but every physician. Every physician leads just by the nature of their responsibilities."

Our leadership team sought to build a culture fortified by strong physician leadership throughout the organization, and the team recognized that there were essential components needed for the best physician leaders. The person had to be highly respected as a clinician and had to possess both keen emotional intelligence and a genuine passion for the work. The physician also had to possess a sense of integrity and humility as well as excellent communication skills and also demonstrate dedication to improvement of self and skills.

The importance of physician as leader was stressed in the medical group's leadership program "Introduction to Management," a two-and-a-half-day course that was conducted quarterly. "We wanted all the physicians to go through this leadership training—those with new administrative roles, experienced physician managers, or physicians who have no formal leadership role," says Fahy, who played a pivotal role. "I would invite new doctors to come to 'Intro to Management' when I saw them in orientation."

My leadership team and I took every opportunity to recognize good work, and we spread supportive news and messages throughout the medical group. We understood at a visceral level that physicians experience a real lift when they are singled out for praise. To any professional, physicians very much included, recognition for one's work is not only uplifting but is also powerfully motivating. A note of praise, a complimentary e-mail, a shout-out at a meeting—these things matter.

This sort of recognition is in critically short supply in health care. In light of the enormous demands and the complexity of the work that doctors face every day, it is increasingly important to recognize and acknowledge the amazing contributions of our best performers—and there were so many in Colorado. Our recognition program was informal, but it was also highly intentional, comprehensive, and sustained over time. In fact, we found that the most impactful positive feedback has three characteristics: it is specific, timely, and linked to our vision and values. There is no question that positive feedback from leadership energizes doctors. Recognition of professional competence and compassion was a powerful currency with our physicians—more powerful in many situations than money.

PLAY TO WIN

An essential component of our learning journey in Colorado came from the KP team in Hawaii. While we were making progress in Colorado, my medical group and health plan colleagues and I all agreed that we needed to do better—to push our performance to another level.

Bill Marsh and Andy Lum learned about the Hawaii work and suggested that we go and take a firsthand look at it to see whether it might be a good fit in Colorado. After significant discussions with my regional health plan partner, our team traveled to Hawaii and found that a program called Play to Win had provided a significant boost to improving work in the region. The program seemed a bit touchy-feely at first, but very quickly I became convinced of its depth and power. Play to Win is a two-and-a-half-day offsite gathering that included a combination of didactic teaching and presentations as well as a more cognitive approach—a results-oriented model. More than that, though, I saw it as a new way of thinking, and I was impressed by how it had helped accelerate change in KP Hawaii.

Perhaps the most concise definition of Play to Win comes from Larry Wilson and Hersch Wilson, coauthors of the book *Play to Win! Choosing Growth over Fear in Work and Life* on which much of the training was based. They write that "in its simplest form, *Playing to Win* is consciously choosing to not automatically avoid situations in which we might fail, be embarrassed, or be rejected. Why on earth would we consciously choose to do something that could lead to failure? Because our goal is to grow. *Playing to Win* is concerned with engaging with life, with the desire to thrive on the adventure. Emotional, spiritual, and intellectual growth are the game's payoff."

The program fascinated my health plan partner and me. After a series of discussions and a fair amount of due diligence, we decided to bring the Play to Win program to the entire region of Colorado. My health plan partner and I believed that we understood both the magnitude of the investment and the challenges we were addressing in the culture of our organization.

Tracy Burke was the facilitator and project manager for the program. "It's about how do we create results in our lives, creating an experience that allows people to get unstuck and think differently," says Burke. "If you want different results you need to do something different, and to do that you need to think differently. We believe resistance to change is emotional, and therefore to help people be more open to change and create change, you have to break through that emotional resistance. The program included personal reflection, conversations as well as experiential exercises."

Predictably, there were a few participants who clung tightly to their steely cynicism, yet for most of the participants the impact of Play to Win was nothing less than profound.

It is a bold promise—that *emotional, spiritual, and intellectual growth are the game's payoff*. And for many at KP Colorado, the program actually fulfilled this promise. The Wilsons teach that fuzzy thinking—that which is little more than an emotional reaction—prevents us from recognizing and taking control of our emotions so that we can think clearly. One of the central elements of the program—a technique called "Stop, Challenge, and Choose"—is designed to teach people how to respond "with more control" under a wide variety of circumstances. The Wilsons write:

> *Stop* is the step of intervening before we respond to an event without thinking. *Challenge* is the step of asking questions: What am I making up that is not based in objective reality? What are other interpretations of this event? *Choose* is the step of selecting a more appropriate interpretation and acting on it. Doing something different in order to influence getting a different result. . . .
>
> *Stop, Challenge, and Choose* is a process that is well-grounded in cognitive psychology and—more important—is highly effective. Just the physical act of stopping and breathing—disconnecting from a tense situation before we respond

in anger—allows us to see more interpretations
and more options than we normally do.

In discussing the "Stop" aspect, the authors write that
"anytime we intervene in our thinking to calm down
and react more consciously, it's usually a good idea. Getting to calm is often the most important part of this process. . . . *Stop* helps us get to calm."

Burke says that overall, Play to Win "provided the
structure for how to go about improving the work experience of staff and physicians, and it signified that invest-
ing in people and teams was the way to do that. . . . Play
to Win laid the foundation for a new level of workforce
engagement."

For some years there had been a natural conflict
between the medical group side of KP and the health plan
side—doctors and insurers tend to tangle whether they
are part of the same organization or not. My health plan
partner and I addressed this natural tension by personally
showing up at virtually every session to reinforce our commitment to the significance of Play to Win in Colorado.

In fact, Play to Win proved to be a useful exercise to
bring the two components of KP Colorado together and
work more harmoniously. Burke says that "while things
were often challenging between the health plan and the
medical group, I think embarking on Play to Win and the
support for it from both sides of the house was a huge
part of the foundation of the transformation. I think it
demonstrated that you knew that the future success of
the organization was dependent on creating an integrated system and on building the capacity of the health
plan and the medical group to partner successfully. . . .
Aligned support for Play to Win was *huge* in sending an
organizational message about collaboration."

The actual content of the Play to Win program, Burke believed, "beautifully supported the transformation. I think there was a huge amount of cynicism in the organization. Play to Win provided a framework for expressing healthy skepticism instead of cynicism. It said there was room for dissent, but you have to be fundamentally committed to the success of the organization."

Amy Edmondson, who worked at Pecos River, the consulting company that created Play to Win, and was an early expert in the program, later went on to accept a faculty position at Harvard Business School, where she remains a staunch believer in the efficacy of Play to Win. Says Edmondson:

It was clear to me that the best theories of learning and personal growth have far more in common than is obvious at first glance. They stem from common wisdom about human cognition and human emotion. Play to Win, which was heavily influenced by the Rational Behavior Therapy tradition, has much in common with the work of Chris Argyris on "defensive routines." Defensive cognitive reasoning is something we use to protect ourselves, but unfortunately it prevents us from learning. This is well understood in several academic and clinical traditions. People try to protect themselves from being wrong, embarrassed, or feeling a lack of control. We want to be in control, but unfortunately that desire often keeps us from learning. We are socialized and hard-wired as humans to do a lot of silly things, without realizing that they're not in our best interest. We think it will make us happy to control others. But it never does, and it makes it hard to learn or innovate.

Play to Win had a powerful emotional impact on many at KP Colorado. One was Dr. Ellsworth (not his real name), a charming, popular physician. But over time, with the toxicity and dysfunction of the medical group, his outlook deteriorated along with that of many other physicians. It was not uncommon for Ellsworth to complain about one aspect of the medical group or another.

But Play to Win penetrated Ellsworth's defenses. One day he said to me, "Jack, a week ago if you'd said I'm going to say this, I would have said you're crazy." Then suddenly, he started to cry. "I've been so angry at Kaiser that I can hardly stand working some days. But what I feel right now is I'm going to stay and I'm going to be proud of this place."

RESULTS AND TURNAROUND

A kind of leadership stew with various mixed ingredients resulted in eye-opening improvements in key performance metrics for our KP Colorado medical group. The stew included the constants, with particular emphasis on preservation and enhancement of career. The doctors found that not only did our leadership team articulate that notion well but that we also backed up our words with actions. Other elements of the stew included the other two constants—optimizing the care experience and streamlining the care process—as well as the healer-leader-partner concept; Play to Win; leadership training, promotion, and measurement; and an aggressive nurse training program.

The turnaround was dramatic:

- Provider satisfaction within the CPMG ("would recommend KP to a friend") took a nosedive, going from 96 percent in 1994 down to 80 percent in 1998. Even worse was the question "would choose CPMG again," where 94 percent said yes in 1994 while 77 percent said yes in 1998. But with a new team in place, significant hard work, and, perhaps more than anything, a cultural shift, we were able to get the satisfaction rates back up to 98 percent in 2002 for "would recommend to a friend" and 95 percent in 2004 for "would choose CPMG again."

- The physician turnover rate declined from 9 percent in 2000 to 2.9 percent in 2005.
- Not surprisingly, along with provider satisfaction rose patient satisfaction. Seeing the patient satisfaction rate improve along with the provider rate was particularly gratifying. Overall patient satisfaction rose from 87 percent in 1995 to 94 percent in 2006.
- KP Colorado was ranked as a "Top 10 Organization" in the HEDIS Effectiveness of Care survey.
- In 2004 HEDIS measures showed KP Colorado to be first in the nation in cholesterol management, second for eye exams for people with diabetes, fourth in cholesterol management screening, and fifth in both lipid control in diabetes and flu shots for patients ages fifty to sixty-five.

Overall, from 1999 to 2007 KP Colorado—the medical group working in cooperation with strong partners from the health plan—increased membership, earned a sustainable margin, and significantly boosted morale. The metrics indicating success were a clear affirmation that the approach our team and our health plan partners had taken had worked. Further affirmation came when leaders of other KP regions recognized the success of the Colorado work. In 2005 an executive from the northern

California region visited Colorado to observe and learn, and after several days she said that there were three significant differences in Colorado. First, in meetings, she was unable to tell who was from the health plan and who was from the medical group. This was a high priority for my health plan partner and me and our teams. Second, she said that every discussion on any topic centered on the patient. And third, she said that it was a can-do atmosphere where everyone talked about getting things done.

Throughout this period, Jeff Pfeffer kept an eye on the results that the organization was achieving. He was impressed with what he saw, so impressed that he wrote a brief article for *Business 2.0* in May 2007 titled "Changing Minds: Most Turnaround Efforts Focus on New Practices or Products; Real Ones Alter How Employees Think about Their Jobs."

And significantly, Pfeffer's view was that the leadership and management at KP Colorado had implications beyond health care. "The story of how CPMG pulled it off carries lessons for almost any struggling company," Pfeffer wrote. He observed that "Many people in health care see the industry as a series of trade-offs: quality vs. cost, patient interests vs. physician interests. The CPMG leadership understood that physician and patient satisfaction and improved financial performance were compatible goals. If doctors experienced better leadership and enjoyed what they were doing, patient care would improve too."

6

The Elephant in the Room

What happens when you have a physician in the group to whom no one will refer?

Too often, the medical culture in the United States tolerates bad behavior by doctors. The culture permits some doctors to be rude, dismissive, and condescending to anyone without an MD after their name. This egocentricity is toxic. What if Dr. Smyth (not his real name) creates an intolerable atmosphere in the clinic? By creating an environment of fear and instability, *patients are at risk.* It's 3 a.m., and a patient is having a problem. The nurse is unsure what to do. She believes that there might be an issue, but she knows that Dr. Smyth is on call and that he can be trouble. The nurse thinks it through: *If I call Smyth at 3 a.m. it could be ugly, so maybe we'll just see if we can get the patient through the night until the hospitalist is on at 7.*

What happens when you have a physician in the group to whom no one will refer? A doctor to whom none of the other physicians will send a family member? If, as a physician, I know enough about Dr. Smyth that I protect my family from him, this means that every fifteen minutes somebody else's family member is coming into Smyth's exam room or that every two hours a patient goes into Smyth's operating room.

Too often doctors steer family, friends, and patients away from that particular physician but ignore the fact that twenty other patients a day are going into the clinic with that same doctor. Why is it that way? Quite often we simply seek to avoid the intense awkwardness of sharply critical conversations with men and women who are friends and colleagues.

For physician group leaders, the question is whether we will tolerate harm on our watch. The answer must always be no, and that is why our leadership team and the board of directors of Colorado Permanente Medical Group (CPMG) took this issue head-on. The fact that Dr. Smyth is not good enough is not necessarily his problem alone—it's *everybody's* problem.

At Kaiser Permanente (KP) Colorado, our first line of defense was to hire great physicians. Yet a few doctors suffered from physician-as-victim syndrome, while others were afflicted with physician-as-tyrant syndrome— two of the least attractive traits in health care.

Our leadership team and board of directors were strongly aligned in supporting doctors in having great careers. We made clear to physicians the need for robust performance appraisal, and we took full responsibility and accountability for oversight of the performance of all physicians in the group, including clinical and team skills.

Throughout their careers, physicians have been continuously tested and measured. After all, every physician went through a challenging undergraduate course of study in the sciences just to be able to make it to medical school. As medical school students, they work to absorb immense amounts of clinical learning. Then comes the rigor of residency. Every step of the way for those ten or more years of education and training, these young men and women are measured on performance. They understand what it means, and in the vast majority of cases they welcome it. For most, it affirms their commitment to excel.

Thus, establishing clear, detailed standards of performance within our medical group and regular performance evaluation came naturally to our physicians because they understood that rigorous physician evaluation is central to providing the best possible patient care. This was the case even though there had been a limited evaluation process.

This did not mean that all physicians reacted well to an evaluation, suggesting that the doctor may need some help to improve in a particular area. Some pushed back. But this is where the difficult conversation is a gift. When you are honest with doctors and your motivation is to help them do a better job for patients, they will work with you.

From the start, our leadership team and the board were animated by a powerful sense that collegiality and professional competence were essential to the functioning of the medical group. I had been steeped in this notion from Jeff Pfeffer at Stanford and naturally gravitated toward it as a way of functioning day-to-day.

A few doctors run into trouble because they fail to keep up with the latest advances in treatments, and as a result, their knowledge and skills erode. When put on a formal performance improvement plan, the great majority of these doctors fairly quickly regain their knowledge and skills. The vast majority of improvement plans created at KP Colorado were highly successful.

With doctors, the more troublesome and complex cases involve citizenship and behavioral issues. *How do you act around patients? Are you a collegial, effective team leader? How do you treat staff members?* We needed physicians to excel in the technical aspects of medicine and in citizenship. In a group practice, good citizenship matters greatly.

"It's not about just being brilliant," says Dr. Bill Wright. "It's not just being at the top of your medical school class. It's how we treat each other."

From the start, we introduced more robust communication to doctors and all staff members and amped up leadership recognition and reward programs while significantly improving communication to all clinicians.

Working with the leadership team, we wrote a comprehensive "Code of Conduct" in December 2000 that made clear what would be the basis for evaluating doctors. As head of human resources, Dr. Patty Fahy played a key role in this work. (In addition, KP nationally has long been guided by its Principles of Responsibility.)

"What we had at the time were the principles of medical practice, which really referred to making decisions based on evidence," says Fahy. "What we didn't have was something that described the kind of behavior and performance expectations we had for physicians."

The Code of Conduct was a foundational document that we sent to applicants for physician positions and used in the performance evaluation and orientation processes. The full "Code of Conduct" can be found in the notes section of this book, and the language makes our goals and values clear noting that physicians will "interact with other physicians, practitioners, and staff . . . in a collegial, supportive and professional manner"; "give feedback to colleagues in a professional manner"; "give corrective feedback to staff in a respectful manner away from patients and other staff"; "express dissenting views in a respectful manner"; and "give candid and timely feedback on peer/staff evaluations."

Many physicians at KP Colorado had personnel files that contained just a slim page or two attesting to their excellence. I referred to these as "Lake Woebegon evaluations"—everyone above average. If an evaluator just comes in and writes "excellent, excellent, exceeds, exceeds" and signs it, that's not an evaluation. *That's an abdication.*

Leadership and the board made a decision early on that we would have a two-step process. First, we would evaluate the doctors. Second, we would *evaluate the quality and rigor of the evaluations.* Had the evaluation been done seriously? Had it been done professionally? Had it been done according to the standards that we had prescribed? The plan was to conduct evaluations on all physicians in the group every year for three years. After that, any doctor with three excellent evaluations in a row would be evaluated every other year.

Throughout this process, my bedrock belief was that the overwhelming majority of physicians who faced challenges could be counseled, receive some training, and be back to providing great care.

Yes, we terminated doctors when we had to. But the goal of our human resources program—achieved in the vast majority of cases—was to improve performance. What could be more patient-centered than actively monitoring and improving the performance of physicians and setting up a robust improvement plan for doctors whose performance had slipped due to a range of factors? If a particular physician had a down period, we wanted to get him or her back on track.

Like other professionals, doctors are human and sometimes hit bumpy patches. If physicians are evaluated with rigor, management discovers those rough patches quickly and can then address them quickly, with positive results nearly every time.

When evaluations reveal that a particular doctor is not performing at the highest level, who is harmed? Patients, of course, but also the physician's colleagues who must pick up the slack or redo the work. Nurses and the rest of the team are also affected, especially when they see standards that have been set but are not being met by a physician. Substandard physician performance harms the credibility of the standards and the credibility of group leadership.

But the low-performing physician is also harmed. Presumably, the doctor has been around the organization long enough to have demonstrated an overall skill as a physician and a team player. Our leadership team and the board believed that we owed it to patients, other physicians, clinical team members, and the low-performing physician to try to find a pathway to improvement. Performance management and improvement efforts are an expression of humanity and concern for the low performer. We are saying to our colleagues who hit bumps along the way, "We care enough about you to not stand by while you are having trouble. We are here to help you get back to doing a great job with patients."

But there are exceptions. Dr. Woodley (not the physician's real name), a new hire, was highly talented and technically proficient. But early on it became clear that Woodley was often condescending and dismissive to staff members. Nothing like this had emerged during the recruitment and orientation periods, yet Woodley was persistently difficult from day one.

Staff members complained, and we—the leadership team—listened. Staffers told us that they were intimidated by Woodley and were routinely belittled, made to feel incompetent. A couple of staff members were so deeply shaken by the mistreatment they received from Woodley that they went on medical leave.

Leaders sat down with Woodley. "This is what we stand for," we said, "and these are our expectations. We told you this when we hired you, and we told you this at orientation. And this is how you're going to get evaluated, and it's not going to go well."

Woodley replied that it was all about efficiency. "I'm just efficient, and if these people are slow, they're going to have to get faster, because I'm efficient."

Efficiency is great, we agreed, but collegiality and effective teamwork are critical as well. We set up a formal performance evaluation and gave Woodley a six-month improvement plan with crystal-clear standards and expectations. Incredibly, the behavior did not change. Woodley continued to abuse staff members, creating a toxic environment in the clinic. So, a high-quality, highly functional clinical doctor who just simply couldn't—or wouldn't—treat staff well was dismissed.

At some places when a doctor is forced to leave, he or she does so quietly. But we felt a responsibility to report Woodley to the National Practitioner Databank, which collects instances of malpractice and other adverse actions related to the professional competence or conduct of practitioners. The information is available to select users, including state licensing boards, hospitals, and other health care entities. Although we know that in some places reporting may be part of the negotiation when a physician is hired or even leaves, that was not our practice. We were not going to sit by and let somebody else evaluate a physician we terminated for serious misconduct without having all the information.

Surgeons cut people open, and when they do so incorrectly the consequences range from serious to catastrophic. All surgeons make mistakes at one time or another during their career. Surgeons react differently to those errors. There was an excellent young surgeon at KP Colorado who made a serious error in his second year of practice and was deeply shaken by it.

Not long after that, he came by my office and said that he felt he had to quit. "I don't think I should do surgery," he told me.

I pointed out that all surgeons make mistakes—certainly I had—and if your first serious error comes at year ten of your career, you already know that for nine years you've been a good surgeon. But when it happens in the first couple of years, doctors sometimes leap to extreme conclusions—that they should not do surgery, for example.

But I knew that he was a talented and insightful surgeon, and I liked the fact that the young man had the humility to question himself in the aftermath of the mistake. I urged him not to quit. "If you have a deficiency in some area, let's have someone scrub in with you," I suggested. "But don't quit," I told him. "Your patients need you." The great thing is that with a little bit of help, he went on to flourish in the operating room.

PARTNERING WITH CLINICAL PHARMACISTS

One of the most tangible benefits of building a new culture of teamwork and respect for one another was the amazing performances by the nurses and clinical pharmacists we partner with. These men and women were diligent and patient-centered all-stars.

In 1993 Dennis Helling, executive director of Pharmacy Operations and Therapeutics for KP Colorado, proposed an innovative new anticoagulation service. Helling wanted to shift supervision of the anticoagulation service from practicing physicians to teams led by clinical pharmacists partnering with a physician. He believed that such a move would reduce the burden of work on physicians, giving them more time to focus on issues that only doctors are capable of handling. The program would also call on clinical pharmacists to work at the top of their licenses. Helling's idea proved to be a real win for patients, physicians, and pharmacists.

"When patients go to a primary care physician and receive a diagnosis of deep vein thrombosis, the patients are typically put on a blood thinner to prevent heart attacks and strokes," says Helling. "But you can also thin the blood too much, and that can be dangerous."

His proposal was that once a physician made such a diagnosis, the patient would be put under the care of a clinical pharmacist who would monitor the patient's condition and make adjustments to medication as needed—with the physician's approval.

When this program was implemented in primary care, it lessened the load on physicians. And while primary care doctors embraced the help, surgeons and cardiologists rejected the proposal. But then Helling showed me the results of his team's work in primary care. When clinical pharmacists managed anticoagulant patients, "we showed a 40 percent reduction in anticoagulation-related morbidity and mortality," Helling said, compared with patients who were not in the program.

I was struck by how great the results were, and I told Helling that "pharmacists do this better than I do." I went to bat for Helling and his team, and we rapidly spread the program.

To me, this was simple—it was about being a good partner to a highly talented group of pharmacists. Leadership is often about modeling the right behavior, and in this case it modeled being a strong team player who recognizes the excellent skills of fellow team members.

Rather than sticking with the reflexive reaction—*as a physician I want to be the one managing my patients' coagulation issues*—I could clearly see that other clinically skilled partners could do the job not only well but also better than most physicians.

When the clinical pharmacy service began to partner with endocrinology and cardiology, clinical pharmacists focused on patients with coronary artery disease who had already suffered a heart attack. Pharmacists monitored the patients' lipid levels and other medications that they took to prevent another heart attack. The result was an 89 percent reduction in mortality.

I had a similar partnership with our nursing staff. One of the most pressing issues confronting the medical group—and all providers—was an acute nursing shortage. Most physician organizations were not actively engaged in solving the many issues related to nursing, but it was clear to me that working to preserve and enhance the careers of nurses was related directly to optimizing the care experience and streamlining the care process. It had been obvious to me from the time I started my training decades earlier that nurses were at the heart of any clinical team. Thus, both the care experience and process relied heavily on the actions and teamwork of skilled nurses.

In the early 2000s when the nursing shortage was at its worst, Linda Smith worked as senior director for

Nursing Services and Quality for KP Colorado. It was a newly created position after a painful nursing strike was settled in 2000. Not surprising, at the heart of the strike was a feeling among nurses that reflected the sense of alienation that was so widespread among doctors.

"There was so much dissatisfaction among the RNs," recalls Smith. "They were feeling they did not have a voice in the company. They were not feeling valued."

Smith took over her new role with a goal of "developing opportunities to inspire nursing excellence, to create career ladders for nurses, and provide ways for advancement." I supported the approach.

I had personal experiences within my family where superb nursing care had played a huge role in the life of a loved one, and I had a real passion to address the nursing shortage. I hired a project manager for nursing issues, and Smith and I worked together to attract quality nurses.

Changing the culture was absolutely essential to solving the nursing shortage for us. There was an abundance of research, including a Veterans Health Administration study that "found that disruptive behavior and verbal abuse was a strong contributing factor to diminished nurse satisfaction and morale. When asked whether they had ever observed abusive behavior by a physician toward a nurse, 96 percent of nurses said yes."

This deeply troubled me, because it was clearly anything but patient-centered. One of the best things that we physicians can do for our patients is to have great working relationships with nurses! Nothing could be more obvious to me. This issue was so central to my view of how to improve patient care that I collaborated with Fahy and our colleague Jill Bansek for an article in

The Permanente Journal in which we wrote that "It is incomprehensible and unacceptable for physicians to be 'silent' on the nursing shortage."

Could there be a group of professionals with any greater stake in solving the nursing shortage than physicians?

- Nurses ensure the quality and safety of care delivered to patients through their scope of practice and technical skills, their culture of empathy and advocacy, and their participation in the development and execution of the patient care plan.
- Nurses extend physician influence and leverage physician time through their expertise in patient education and their management of other health care team members.
- Nurses partner with physicians, anticipating difficulties in patient care, offering options, working with family members, and optimizing communication in the care of patients.

Working with the Community College of Denver, our KP team developed a program for medical assistants at KP to go to school to earn the licensed practical nurse (LPN) certification. We provided funding, a location for the instruction, and a place for the clinical rotation. All of this was free of charge to the students.

We also created a program where individuals with a bachelor's degree could earn a B.S.R.N. in 18 months. My KP colleague Marilyn Chow, RN, who currently serves as vice president of National Patient Care Services at KP, played an important role as one of my key health plan partners in this work. We created and funded a program at Metro State College that enabled men and women with bachelor degrees to earn RN certification in just eighteen months. Notably, this program was not just for KP employees but was open to anyone in the community. We also funded nursing simulation laboratories—excellent facilities for high-level nurse training—at Regis University and another at Metro State College. With a faculty shortage in nurse training programs, these simulation laboratories proved particularly valuable.

7

Turnaround

We were making progress, and it was clear to me that the most important measure of that progress was not a particular metric but rather a cultural evolution that generated a new sense of identity within our Colorado group. Signs of a more collegial, respectful culture were everywhere, and the concept of preservation and enhancement of physician careers seemed to echo throughout the organization.

An important part of the cultural shift was a by-product of our leadership team's intentional and sustained effort to identify throughout the organization a group of what we called signal generators—particularly well-respected clinicians who were thoughtful, influential, and highly respected by their peers. Our leadership team identified approximately one hundred individuals throughout Kaiser Permanente (KP) Colorado who were recruited as signal generators. Each of us on the executive team was assigned to connect and meet monthly with about a dozen of the signal generators to answer questions and provide insights into policy decisions. This proved to be an effective way to stay connected to the front lines. On a deeper level, however, over time this process and these relationships between senior leaders and signal generators created a more open, cooperative, and trusting culture throughout KP Colorado.

Leaders communicate in different ways. There is the classic connectivity between senior leaders and their direct reports, and there is a greater need for leaders to listen to everyone in the organization. Between those two levels is the opportunity for leaders to connect closely with a variety of men and women who do not hold formal leadership titles but who, because they are widely respected by their peers, are actually powerful forces within the organization. These are highly credible people whom everybody in the organization seems to respect and listen to. Susan may not hold an official leadership title, but when important issues arise, you hear people asking, "What does Susan think about this?" Signal generators were not only excellent clinicians but also had the ability, as Patty Fahy put it, to "transform somebody's day for the better, to transform a department because they joined it, because they have fabulous skills, and because the staff really enjoyed working with them."

Leadership may appear logical and straightforward: focus intensively on the right priorities, and things will click into place. But I found that leadership had all the unpredictability and complexity of a Rubik's Cube in the hands of a novice. To me, connecting dots was a logical and rational exercise, but it was quite different from managing the daily reality of highly complex and highly skilled independent human beings. My central lesson about leadership that emerged over time was that the challenge of leading competent, individual souls is not about logic or compulsion. It's about listening, respect, relentless adherence to values, and sticking to that approach every day—an approach that goes a long way toward repairing a wounded culture.

These advances in our culture proved foundational to setting the stage for one of the toughest practical tests we would face: the rapid installation of a new electronic health record (EHR) throughout KP Colorado.

Clinicians generally dread the installation of new information technology systems, and with good reason. New systems disrupt their practice, take time away from patients, unsettle many staff members, and require extensive training. Installing a new EHR too often becomes a tug-of-war. The clinical and administrative staffs from both the medical group and the health plan complain that the administration is forcing this on us, while administrators wring their hands at what they perceive to be the recalcitrance of the staff.

In a way, installing an EHR is an acid test of an organization's culture and management. We had a seven-year-old system that had served the organization well, yet it clearly needed to be replaced.

In the fall of 2005, our team needed to install a new EHR system throughout KP Colorado. This required training more than five hundred doctors and other clinicians as well as hundreds of employees and doing so across twenty-two sites. We were prepared for this undertaking in large measure due to the significant shifts in culture we had worked on for years. While the installation of the new EHR happened in 2005, foundational work to make it possible began much earlier.

I acknowledged that in most cases on day one of EHR installation the physicians would be slowed down and that costs would increase, but I also knew that there would be significant rewards from getting a great system in place.

As the final stage of planning started, I wondered what effective leadership would look like in such a situation. As I discussed this with my senior team, it became clear that a leadership prerequisite was for the senior executive team to roll up our sleeves alongside our colleagues. We had to clear our desks and schedules and head out to the front lines of care to serve as teachers, guides, and mentors. Working closely with my colleagues in the medical group and our partners in the health plan, we came up with an approach that built upon our cultural advances to date and proved particularly effective.

Health care workers are not easily persuaded that a new technology that will disrupt their lives and nudge many of them well outside their comfort zones is worthwhile, particularly when everyone in the organization is already working at peak capacity! That is why preparation—laying the groundwork—was so critical.

In essence, we took four steps in the installation of a great new EHR system. First, we mounted a rigorous effort to go out and share information about the need for the change. We wanted people to understand the reality of the current state. We provided detailed context so that it gradually became clear that there was in fact a strong case to be made for installing a new EHR system. We were crystal clear in our goal: we needed a new system to better care for patients and to make the work of all providers and staff more efficient and patient-centered. Convincing people of this does not happen easily or quickly. This is not about oracular pronouncements. This is about relying on the power of our substantive case and on the communications network we had built throughout Colorado.

For many months prior to going live, our senior team made a consistent and ultimately compelling case to the physicians, other clinicians, and health plan staff that the existing KP Colorado EHR system was preventing us from reaching our full potential. We pressed our case that while the transition would be difficult, it would be more than worth the effort. In the end, we argued, the new EHR system would enable clinicians to provide better patient care.

This first step—*context sharing*—cannot be rushed. There are no shortcuts at this stage of the process. It must be done carefully, steadily, and with great discipline. There is no silver bullet. Convincing very busy people working under pressure that such a disruptive change is necessary does not happen overnight. It requires Professor Randall Root's thinking: *If we both have the same information, it is more likely that we will come to a mutually agreeable solution.* Context sharing in our case involved hundreds of conversations—one on one as well as in small groups and large groups. It involved listening and acknowledging the legitimacy of concerns that others held. This is not a single convincing speech or communication. Rather, it is about a commitment to an iterative communication journey of sharing, proposing, listening, reacting, and learning to arrive at a shared understanding of what reality truly looks like and why change is essential.

If leaders have established a track record of listening and demonstrating a willingness to be influenced by others, as we had in Colorado, it advances the cause. There is a sense of respect, a belief among staff that the *leaders have been straight shooters for the past few years. They have not tried to bully us or force anything down our throats and are being straight shooters on this matter.*

Many thoughtful people have written about change leadership as a separate discipline, but I learned from this major EHR implementation project that all leadership is about leading change.

The second step involved providing adequate resources for change. This means recognizing and respecting the fact that people are very busy and focused on their daily work. Asking them to take on a difficult change without the proper backup and breathing room is counterproductive. Resources are required for time and planning, for training, and for covering all necessary bases with backup workers when necessary. The idea is not to squeeze in training that is barely adequate in the hope of getting things done quickly and cheaply. The goal is to provide the time, training, and support that allows everyone who works with the new EHR to learn and ultimately master the technology and enhance patient care.

On the surface it appears that this approach adds significant cost to the change effort, and certainly it is an expensive undertaking. But in fact, it is truly an investment with significant improvements in efficiency, quality, and the care experience by optimizing the potential of the system.

When the basic groundwork to prepare for change is done and the organization is ready for the change, the next step is to identify the early adopters who are most likely to embrace the system, use it effectively, and serve as models for others.

All four steps toward a successful implementation of a new EHR are important, but this one—identifying early adopters for change—proved to be a key element of this effort. These men and women with energetic can-do attitudes are physicians, nurses, administrators, and others who have demonstrated enthusiasm and a desire for this improvement.

The early adopters are special people. They are bright, confident men and women who are not intimidated by a trip outside their comfort zone, and they do not believe that just because something has been done a certain way for years means that it must hold true in perpetuity. They are thoughtful and open-minded but are also demanding and questioning and thus have strong credibility among their peers.

One of the keys to the success of our installation was making sure we identified the *right* early adopters who provided a nucleus of influential, skilled users who became part of a relay team. We focused on one clinic where we knew the team would enthusiastically embrace the new EHR and then be able to help spread knowledge and enthusiasm throughout the rest of our organization. Why were these men and women so crucial to the success of the rollout? Because once the early adopter clinics go live and the social networks are buzzing, the opinions of the early adopters *will be more credible to the rest of the organization than almost anything management can say.*

Assuming that one has done all the previous steps correctly and resourced this group well—and we had done that in Colorado—there should be a high likelihood that the early adopters will be able to carry a strong, positive message throughout the organization.

We would never have been as successful as we were without the work of these early adopters who also served as our signal generators. But it must be said that the leadership team played an important role as well. While a variety of training options were offered to all employees—small classes, instructional DVDs, training online—there was something powerful about senior leaders sitting down next to a physician, a nurse, or a medical assistant and walking that person through the new system with confidence and detailed knowledge.

Bill Marsh recalls that "everybody on the leadership team canceled our appointments, and we went out into the field for five weeks working side by side with the content experts" from Epic, the company providing the basic EHR system that we would build upon and install. The Epic system was quite strong, but we made it even better by customizing it to create KP HealthConnect—a robust EHR system that included interfaces to multiple non-Epic systems. The rapid installation required that all the leaders learn the Epic system well in advance so that we would have the capability of answering common questions and help with the installation. This required that we—the leadership team—be ready for the inevitable frustration that physicians and other clinicians felt during the early stages of the installation of KP HealthConnect.

Why are the opinions of these early adopters/signal generators so widely respected? Because they do not hold official leadership positions and can express themselves more freely. In our superconnected social world today, signal generators can greatly influence and accelerate change. They are the team members with the greatest "street cred."

Speed does not come from going fast. Speed is a product of following these foundational steps and building credibility and trust that generate momentum. Speed is a product of that momentum.

The fourth and final step accelerates the power of relay teams throughout the organization. This step leverages all of the carefully executed first three phases, thus enabling our bands of signal generators/early adopters to travel to subsequent clinics to lead and model change; to teach, guide, and counsel; to reassure those who are reluctant to change; and to make the installation work.

At this stage in our work in Colorado, there was a buzz from multiple sources that the process had been validated and that it worked. At that juncture we had the momentum necessary to push forward with complete implementation.

The cultural change, the planning, and the groundwork all paid off beautifully in the end, for we accomplished something quite extraordinary in health care: we installed a new EHR system in Colorado in warp speed—from training to going live in just four weeks and two days!

PART III
Pathway Forward

---

*Solving the Doctor Crisis, Expanding
the Learning Coalition*

8

Solving the Physician Crisis While Expanding the Learning Coalition

The Quadruple Aim

We have an idea of what the future looks like.

During the past decade, three overriding aspirations have helped define the foundational goals in American health care. The first emerged from *Crossing the Quality Chasm: A New Health System for the 21st Century*, the landmark Institute of Medicine report that challenged health care stakeholders to deliver care that is "safe, effective, patient-centered, timely, efficient, and equitable."

The second aspiration, framed by Drs. Don Berwick and John Whittington, along with their Institute of Healthcare Improvement colleague Tom Nolan, defined "true north" in health care as the "Triple Aim"—improving the patient experience of care (including quality and satisfaction) while simultaneously improving the health of populations and reducing the per capita cost of care. The third aspiration is the historic challenge to provide robust health insurance to all Americans.

Taken together, these metagoals define a consensus aspiration: high-quality, accessible, affordable care for all. Getting there will require two interrelated, foundational prerequisites: solving the physician crisis to ensure strong, responsible physician leaders and inclusion of all health care stakeholders to expand the Learning Coalition.

As we noted earlier, the Learning Coalition is a collection of individuals and organizations that *exist within the fabric of health care*—a growing, organic force where physicians and other caregivers come together to identify and solve common problems. At its core is an effort to spread the best learning—to turn the best work *anywhere* into the standard *everywhere*.

The Learning Coalition and the physician crisis are deeply interrelated whereby the coalition consists of active physicians practicing in an environment where systems and teams encourage and allow doctors to put the patients' needs above all else. When this happens, physician satisfaction rates soar. Expanding and enhancing the Learning Coalition will solve a major part of the physician crisis. Therefore, it is essential that health care become a world-class learning industry.

It is our experience—and the experience of many physicians with whom we have worked and spoken—that doctors actively engaged in the Learning Coalition have higher levels of professional satisfaction and efficacy because they are involved with change and improvement and accept the expanded role of the physician as healer-leader-partner to find better solutions for their patients, thereby reducing doctors' sense of frustration in the face of bureaucratic obstacles.

Patients need doctors to come off the sidelines on a wide variety of issues ranging from primary care to liability reform, from payment methods to access, and from the uses of technology to the challenge of disparities. Physicians are often effective at aggregating around self-interest via national or local organizations that lobby on behalf of the interests of all doctors or particular specialty groups, but patients need physicians to aggregate around *their* interests. Greater participation in the Learning Coalition throughout the country is an essential component of solving both the physician crisis and the overall health care challenge in the United States.

What does it look like when doctors adopt the role of healer-leader-partner? When they join together with other caregivers to innovate on behalf of patients? When they expand the knowledge of the Learning Coalition? It looks very much like work conducted by Drs. Christine A. Sinsky and Tom Bodenheimer and their associates and detailed in the *Annals of Family Medicine* (May–June 2013) in an article titled "In Search of Joy in Practice: A Report of 23 High-Functioning Primary Care Practices." To emphasize the point about improving the plight of physicians, Sinsky and her associates observe that "physician fulfillment in daily work is tightly related to the organization of the practice environment, including relief from paperwork and administrative hassles, the opportunity to form meaningful relationships with patients, and the ability to provide high-quality care to patients." (For a list of the twenty-three sites, see Annals of Family Medicine, Appendix 1, http://www.annfammed.org /content/11/3/272/suppl/DC1.)

In their report, Sinsky and her colleagues highlight "innovations gathered from high-functioning primary care practices, innovations we believe can facilitate joy in practice and mitigate physician burnout." Visiting twenty-three "high-performing primary care practices," the Sinsky team "focused on how these practices distribute functions among the team, use technology to their advantage, improve outcomes with data, and make the job of primary care feasible and enjoyable as a life's vocation."

This is the Learning Coalition in action! The "In Search of Joy in Practice" report observed that

those who practice adult primary care are often deeply dissatisfied, spending much of their days performing functions that do not require their professional training. More than one-half of general internists and family physicians have symptoms of burnout. Time pressure, chaotic work environments, increasing administrative and regulatory demands, an expanding knowledge base, fragmentation of care delivery, and greater expectations placed on primary care contribute to the strain. Workdays are getting longer and rewards are diminishing. Joy is in short supply.

In this context, the authors "propose *joy in practice* as a deliberately provocative concept to describe what we believe is missing in the physician experience of primary care."

The authors note that "joy in practice includes a high level of physician work life satisfaction, a low level of burnout, and a feeling that medical practice is fulfilling. Physicians who dread going to work each day are not experiencing joy in practice."

The report continues:

The current practice model in primary care is unsustainable. We question why young people would devote 11 years preparing for a career during which they will spend a substantial portion of their work days, as well as much of their personal time at nights, on form-filling, box-ticking, and other clerical tasks that do not utilize their training. Likewise, we question whether patients benefit when their physicians spend most of their work effort on such tasks. Primary care physician burnout threatens the quality of patient care, access, and cost-containment within the US health care system.

Sinsky, Bodenheimer, and their colleagues are powerful examples of physicians who have rejected the notion of sitting on the sidelines and have joined forces to seek a better way by pursuing approaches and techniques that will advance physician satisfaction. They have gone out in search of what Don Berwick calls the "gems," those places where healer-leader-partner physicians find new and better ways to treat patients and simultaneously improve patient care and professional satisfaction for physicians. Sinsky, Bodenheimer, and their colleagues found multiple examples of innovations in practices that support the physician with excellent teamwork—and with team members working at the top of their licenses. Thus, physicians are able to focus their abilities on patient concerns, not only improving patient care but also "enhancing physician joy in practice."

"In Search of Joy in Practice" reports on an array of approaches that hit their target of quality care for patients and higher satisfaction for physicians. Many of these are small changes, but their synergistic power is great. Among some of the most effective practices the team identified are:

- Proactive planned care, with previsit planning and previsit laboratory tests;
- Sharing clinical care among a team, with expanded rooming protocols, standing orders, and panel management;
- Sharing clerical tasks with collaborative documentation (scribing), nonphysician order entry, and streamlined prescription management; and
- Improving communication by verbal messaging and in-box management.

Dr. Bodenheimer and his University of California San Francisco colleague Rachel Willard made a valuable contribution to "In Search of Joy in Practice," conducting seven of the twenty-three primary care site visits covered in the report. After studying the seven practices, Bodenheimer and Willard authored a paper titled "The Building Blocks of High-Performing Primary Care: Lessons from the Field" for the California Health Care Foundation in which they observed that primary care in the United States "is undergoing a transformation—from physician-centered practices to patient-focused teams." Bodenheimer believes so strongly in the importance of clinician morale that, he says, "the Triple Aim should be a quadruple aim, with clinician and staff satisfaction a necessity to achieve the other three aims."

Bodenheimer and Willard's visits to the seven primary care clinics were to better understand how they adapted their practices to put the patient at the center. Their report focuses on ten building blocks that resulted in "increased satisfaction among patients and clinic staff, positive clinical quality metrics, and improved financial stability":

1. Engaged leadership, including patients, creating a practice-wide vision with concrete objectives and goals.
2. Data-driven improvement using computer-based technology. (Performance data are used in all corners of the organization to spur effective action).
3. Empanelment and panel size management: Patients are assigned to a clinician, and clinics actively manage panel size, balancing capacity with demand.
4. Team-based care:
   a. Culture shift: Share the Care,
   b. Stable teamlets,
   c. Colocation,
   d. Staffing ratios adequate to facilitate new roles,
   e. Standing orders/protocols,
   f. Defined workflows and workflow mapping, and
   g. Communication, including daily huddles and minute-to-minute interactions.
5. Patient-team partnership:
   a. Evidence-based care;
   b. Health coaching;
   c. Informed, activated patients; and
   d. Shared decision making.
6. Population management:
   a. Panel management,
   b. Self-management support (health coaching), and
   c. Complex care management.

7. Continuity of care.
8. Prompt access to care:
    a. Weekday hours,
    b. Nights/weekends, and
    c. Phone access.
9. Comprehensiveness and care coordination:
    a. Within the medical neighborhood, and
    b. With community partners, and
    c. With family and caregivers.
10. Template of the future: Escape from the fifteen-minute visit:
    a. E-visits,
    b. Phone visits,
    c. Group visits,
    d. Visits with nurses and other team members, and
    e. Payment reform.

The work by Drs. Sinsky, Bodenheimer, and their colleagues is instructive and inspiring, for they have broken out of the narrow definition of a physician as healer and embraced the concept of physician as healer-leader-partner. In doing so, they have taken on broad accountability for their patients' health care, going beyond the clinic in search of improvements and joining together with others in a collaborative process that enhances the strength and power of their recommendations. They have identified improvements that seek to summon the idealist and enable the healer in all physicians to alleviate suffering and save lives.

There was this incredible disconnect between how primary care was being treated and the value it creates.

Not only are more and more established physicians in clinics and hospitals stepping forward in this manner, but so too are increasing numbers of medical students and residents. Dr. Andrew Morris-Singer is a good example. In 2010 Harvard Medical School made the decision to defund its primary care program, which elicited a strong response from some faculty and students as well as some hospitals associated with the medical school.

A number of students, residents, and faculty "were really upset," says Morris-Singer, who was a resident at the time. "Defunding the division of primary care made no sense, especially at a time when the Affordable Care Act was coming down the line and millions of Americans would have coverage but no physicians, given the primary care physician shortage. What was Harvard thinking?"

Dr. Dave Gellis, a fifth-year student at the time, worked with fellow classmates to put together an online petition seeking support for the primary care program, and within a week it had attracted more than a thousand signatures. This ignited a movement. Morris-Singer, Gellis, and other colleagues worked to convene a campus town hall meeting, where they made the case that Harvard could play a significant leadership role in strengthening primary care in the country.

While this discussion was going on, lightning struck: an anonymous donor offered thirty million dollars to establish a Center for Primary Care at Harvard Medical School with the mission of engaging a wide variety of stakeholders to identify innovations and train leaders in pursuit of advancing primary care. Thus, Harvard went from defunding its primary care program to embracing a center on primary care innovation that aims to be a world leader. And this happened because a few medical students, faculty members, and residents (and a remarkably generous donor) stood up and said, "No, our patients need us to stay in the primary care game in a serious way." These students, faculty, and residents are classic examples of physicians as healers-leaders-partners— going beyond the traditions of the exam room to fight for what they believe is in the best interest of their patients.

As impressive as this was, there's more. Morris-Singer, who had a background as a community organizer before enrolling at Harvard, saw an opportunity to spread the work to other campuses. As the issue was being debated at Harvard, he and other organizers heard from students and residents at other medical schools.

"They wanted to be part of the transformation of primary care," Morris-Singer says. "There was this incredible disconnect between how primary care was being treated and the value it creates. It was a perfect moment of misalignment and pain and passion in the primary care community, and we thought if we could get the people who felt this way moving in the same way, it could be powerful."

In 2010 Morris-Singer and Gellis, along with other colleagues, launched a new organization called Primary Care Progress "to bring together people who were not only passionate about primary care but also willing to consider a new way of going about effecting change." Morris-Singer's belief was that "a direct grassroots approach empowers primary care clinicians on the front lines. Our approach draws on community organizing with a field organizing model that engages clinicians, trainees, and educators from family medicine, pediatrics, internal medicine, and our teams help them with advocacy training, leadership development, and more."

Within three years, the organization grew to include twenty-six active chapters with a dozen more in formation.

Morris-Singer says that the organization has tapped into a rich vein of discontent among many different providers who are eager to find more effective ways of delivering primary care. Primary Care Progress teams have trained hundreds of health care professionals in basic organizing and leadership skills to be able to promote innovation in primary care. "We train them, and we connect people so they can learn from one another," says Morris-Singer. "They give each other ideas and hope."

Among the most notable and effective members of the Learning Coalition is Dr. Gary Kaplan at Virginia Mason Medical Center in Seattle. Kaplan and his colleagues have been among the world leaders in adapting the principles and tools of the Toyota Production System to health care. Their improved metrics over the past dozen years demonstrate the enormous power of this lean management approach to improving quality, safety, access, and affordability. Change in health care—especially change aimed at a significant cultural shift—takes courage. When Kaplan first proposed adapting the Toyota Production System to health care in 2001, he was sharply criticized by leading doctors and administrators within his own organization. Yet he pressed forward with the support of a strong team and the full support of the Virginia Mason Board. He and the team saw firsthand the remarkable efficiency and quality of the Toyota production lines in Japan.

The Virginia Mason Medical Center has achieved significant financial success. The organization is widely recognized as one of the safest health care systems in the country, and one result of that has been a striking 74 percent decline in the cost of liability insurance since 2005. On an array of critical metrics, Virginia Mason has demonstrated improved quality, safety, access, and affordability.

The success of Kaplan and his team has been so pronounced that thousands of health care professionals from throughout the nation and more than twenty foreign countries have traveled to Seattle to learn from Virginia Mason teams. The demand has been so great that Kaplan established the Virginia Mason Institute to teach others in health care what Kaplan and his colleagues have learned.

As noted above, Tom Bodenheimer's important work adds significantly to the concept of the physician as healer-leader-partner, particularly his idea to add physician and staff satisfaction to the Triple Aim. Bodenheimer has also taken on one of the most vexing challenges facing health care in the United States: the alarming prospect of a shortage of primary care physicians. In a November 2013 article in *Health Affairs* titled "Primary Care: Proposed Solutions to the Physician Shortage without Training More Physicians," Bodenheimer and Mark D. Smith, former president and CEO of the California HealthCare Foundation, outlined a thoughtful approach to solving the primary care challenge www.healthaffairs.org.

Bodenheimer and Smith argue that looking to solve the shortage under the current model is doomed to fail and that adding large numbers of primary care physicians in a relatively short time is unrealistic. However, they write that "primary care capacity can be greatly increased without many more clinicians: by empowering licensed personnel, including registered nurses and pharmacists, to provide more care; by creating standing orders for non-licensed health personnel, such as medical assistants, to function as panel managers and health coaches to address many preventive and chronic care needs; by increasing the potential for more patient self-care; and by harnessing technology to add capacity." Their case is bolstered by the alarming possibility that "by 2016 the number of adult primary care physicians *leaving practice will exceed the number entering*" (emphasis added).

Bodenheimer and Smith frame their case in a compelling fashion. The primary care challenge, they contend, is "mislabeled as a physician workforce shortage. The accurate formulation is a demand-capacity mismatch. Primary care practices could greatly increase their capacity to meet patient demand if they reallocate clinical responsibilities—with the help of current technologies—to nonphysician team members and to patients themselves."

If everyone on the team works at the top of his or her license, it becomes possible to redistribute tasks that burden a physician to other team members, leaving the doctor to do the kind of work for which physicians are trained. And this in turn results in greater satisfaction for patients and physicians. Nurses, "pharmacists, psychologists, licensed clinical social workers, physical and occupational therapists, and health educators," Bodenheimer and Smith write, can play a much larger role. "These highly skilled professionals are seriously underused in their capacity to fill roles generally performed by clinicians. Nonlicensed health care personnel—medical assistants, front desk staff, health coaches, patient navigators, and lay educators—are equally underused."

Bodenheimer is a prime example of a physician who has chosen the role of healer-leader-partner. He is an active, dynamic member of the Learning Coalition.

The same can be said of Dr. Peter Pronovost, director of the Armstrong Institute for Patient Safety and Quality at Johns Hopkins. Pronovost's passion for improving patient safety drove him to come up with a simple checklist to reduce the chances of patients developing infections while in the intensive care unit. At Johns Hopkins, implementation of the checklist, according to a 2007 *New Yorker* article by Dr. Atul Gawande, resulted in improvements "so dramatic" that Pronovost and his colleagues were uncertain "whether to believe them: the ten-day line-infection rate went from eleven per cent to zero." Gawande notes that over the following year or so, there were just two line infections!

Pronovost subsequently worked with the Michigan Hospital Association to help spread the approach to every hospital in that state, and within a matter of months the rate of infection in intensive care units in Michigan plunged by 66 percent. Pronovost has become one of the most passionate and effective patient-safety advocates in the nation. His safety checklist approach to preventing infections has all but eliminated central line catheter infections in Michigan and has been adopted by hundreds of other health care organizations throughout the nation.

Among the most influential healer-leader-partner physicians are those many doctors who worked with a wide variety of professional societies to create the Choosing Wisely initiative. This program, which is now spreading throughout the nation, holds the promise of improving care standards by eliminating billions of dollars in unnecessary treatments. One physician who stood up and made an eloquent case for change—Dr. Howard Brody—triggered this enormous achievement.

Dr. Brody serves as director of the Institute for the Medical Humanities and professor of family medicine at the University of Texas Medical Branch.

In January 2010 Brody published an article in the *New England Journal of Medicine* titled "Medicine's Ethical Responsibility for Health Care Reform—The Top Five List" that sparked the Choosing Wisely initiative. In his article, Brody proposed

> that each specialty society commit itself immediately to appointing a blue-ribbon study panel to report, as soon as possible, that specialty's "Top Five" list . . . five diagnostic tests or treatments that are very commonly ordered by members of that specialty, that are among the most expensive services provided, and that have been shown by the currently available evidence not to provide any meaningful benefit to at least some major categories of patients for whom they are commonly ordered. In short, the Top Five list would be a prescription for how, within that specialty, the most money could be saved most quickly without depriving any patient of meaningful medical benefit. . . .
>
> Having once agreed on the Top Five list, each specialty society should come up with an implementation plan for educating its members as quickly as possible to discourage the use of the listed tests or treatments for specified categories of patients. Umbrella organizations such as the AMA [American Medical Association] might push hard on specialty societies and pressure the laggards to step up.

The National Physicians Alliance, *Consumer Reports*, and the American Board of Internal Medicine (ABIM) accelerated the Choosing Wisely initiative. The ABIM Foundation, under the healer-leader-partner leadership of Dr. Christine K. Cassel, then demonstrated precisely the kind of vision and leadership that can help improve the quality and affordability of care. The foundation created the Choosing Wisely initiative "to promote conversations between physicians and patients by helping patients choose care that is supported by evidence, not duplicative of other tests or procedures already received, free from harm, truly necessary."

Examples of guidelines include the following:

- From the American Academy of Neurology: "Don't perform electroencephalography (EEG) for headaches." "Don't perform imaging of the carotid arteries for simple syncope without other neurologic symptoms." "Don't use opioid or butalbital treatment for migraine except as a last resort."
- From the American Academy of Orthopaedic Surgeons: "Avoid performing routine post-operative deep vein thrombosis ultrasonography screening in patients who undergo elective hip or knee arthroplasty."
- From the American College of Cardiology: "Don't perform stress cardiac imaging or advanced noninvasive imaging in the initial evaluation of patients without cardiac symptoms unless high-risk markers are present."
- From the American Society of Clinical Oncology: "Don't perform PET, CT, and radionuclide bone scans in the staging of early breast cancer at low risk for metastasis."

The spread of the initiative has been nothing short of remarkable. Since the launch in 2010, more than fifty specialty societies have chosen to participate. In addition, *Consumer Reports* publishes material about the procedures on its lists to help patients engage in richer, more productive conversations *about what is right for them* with their doctors.

During an interview with Dr. Pauline Chen for the *New York Times* ("The Doctor's Failure to Cut Costs," March 4, 2010), Brody spoke to the broader responsibilities that physicians have—a clear echo of the healer-leader-partner concept. Doctors "have a moral duty as an individual advocate," he said. "A doctor has a responsibility to his or her individual patients to make them healthier and to help them live longer. But doctors have a second moral duty: they have an obligation to the general public to be prudent stewards of scarce resources."

We have an idea of what the future looks like.

Among leading physicians propelling the Learning Coalition forward is Dr. Paul Grundy, director of Healthcare Transformation at IBM.

Grundy wears many hats in his fevered and relentless pursuit of quality and value for all patients. He is, among many other things, the founder and president of the Patient-Centered Primary Care Collaborative, where he and his colleagues are among the most thoughtful and articulate advocates for the effectiveness of the patient-centered medical home—a primary care location that is patient-centered, comprehensive, team-based, coordinated, accessible, and focused on quality and safety.

Grundy and his colleagues at the Patient-Centered Primary Care Collaborative suggest that there is a "consensus across the health care marketplace and political spectrum that patient-centered, coordinated, team-based primary care is critical to achieving a high-value health care system." Key recommendations by the group are aimed at supporting "the alignment of major public policy priorities and private sector innovations" and include the following:

> Payment reform incentives for providers, consumers, employers, and states that reward shifts toward high-value, high-quality delivery models such as medical homes, Accountable Care Organizations (ACOs), and integrated health systems.
>
> New delivery models that maximize innovations in care, particularly for high-need, high-risk populations, and the further expansion of high-value models such as medical homes and ACOs.
>
> Patient and consumer engagement strategies that incentivize consumers and patients to make high-value choices, and enable smarter choices through the availability of free tools, resources, and patient health data.

In 2006 Grundy was approached by IBM's Dr. Martin Sepulveda, who had just read an article titled "Primary Care—Will It Survive?" in the *New England Journal of Medicine* by Tom Bodenheimer about the power of primary care. As they discussed and studied the issue, it was clear to both Dr. Grundy and Dr. Sepulveda that "where there was robust, proactive primary care with teams managing populations, we were having much greater success," says Grundy. "It was so clear that going forward we would have to manage a population of patients with a plan for every patient. And it was clear that three things were driving this. Unsustainable cost was one. Another was

that for the first time in history we have the data we
need to manage populations. And third we had entered
a whole new era of communication and technology."

In recognizing these trends, Grundy and Sepulveda
envisioned the need for an organization that would
advance the cause of primary care in general and the primary care home in particular. IBM and thought-leaders
from throughout the world of primary care, along with
a number of insurance companies, convened a meeting.
Organized groups representing family doctors, internists,
pediatricians, and osteopaths were asked to "agree on a
set of principles that we could focus on at the micro level
and we—employers and payers—would support at the
macro level in payment," says Grundy. Examples of the
principles include:

- Personal physician. Each patient has an ongoing
  relationship with a personal physician trained to
  provide first contact, continuous, and comprehensive care.
- Physician-directed medical practice. The personal
  physician leads a team of individuals at the practice level who collectively take responsibility for
  the ongoing care of patients.
- Whole-person orientation. The personal physician is responsible for providing for all the patient's
  health care needs or taking responsibility for appropriately arranging care with other qualified professionals. This includes care for all stages of life: acute
  care, chronic care, preventive services, and end-of-
  life care.
- Care is coordinated and/or integrated across all elements of the complex health care system (subspe-
  cialty care, hospitals, home health agencies, nursing

homes) and the patient's community (family, public, and private community-based services). Care
is facilitated by registries, information technology,
health information exchange, and other means to
ensure that patients get the indicated care when
and where they need and want it in a culturally
and linguistically appropriate manner.

The principles led to a series of primary care pilot programs intended to improve quality and control costs.
Thus was launched an important coalition between
major U.S. corporations and a variety of primary care
providers. Initially in 2006 there were eighteen medical
home pilots, all of which achieved a high degree of success. Today there are hundreds of pilots throughout the
country. As Grundy points out, "Many if not most of the
organizations that started out with pilots have decided
that this approach works, and they are going ahead with
it. If you put resources upstream—if you manage aspirin, blood pressure, and cholesterol upstream you have
a third less need to do cardiac intervention. If you don't
manage those things, you see more cardiac disease. This
isn't rocket science!"

The pilot projects consistently achieved a 9–10 percent
decline in the number of patients going to Emergency
Departments and a 20–30 percent decline in patients
hospitalized for ambulatory sensitive conditions. Grundy
estimates that currently about 18 percent of primary care
practices in the nation are in a medical home category
(National Committee for Quality Assurance [NCQA] certified or other), and he predicts that this number will rise
rapidly in the years to come. Increasingly, health plans
and employers are "declaring this their standard of care.
So you have to do it because payers are demanding it."

And the payers not only include large employers but also government entities, including the Centers for Medicare and Medicaid Services, the U.S. Office of Personnel Management (nine million lives under age sixty-five and retired federal employees), and TriCare, which covers benefits for service people and their families in the U.S. military. The results of the primary care home work during the past half dozen or so years has Grundy feeling a sense of excitement about the future. "We have an idea," he says, "of what the future looks like."

A more efficient future pathway will require better tools for physicians. Grundy talks about how much time physicians are forced to waste writing patient data into the electronic health record and notes that technology will solve that problem in the years to come by recording the physician-patient conversation and integrating it instantly into the health record.

A new technology with immense potential is already emerging in the form of Watson, the IBM computer made famous for its ability to outgun even the most elite players on the television program *Jeopardy*. Watson's capability is to examine all of the literature related to a particular disease, for example, and deliver pinpoint information at the point of care.

"Watson is cognitive," says Grundy. "In less than three seconds, Watson can sift through two hundred million pages of research and provide a clear response at the point of care. It has the ability to identify a patient's specific circumstances and pinpoint the most effective treatment to the doctors and nurses on the care team—in seconds. With medical information doubling about every five years, the doctor is no longer the data storage repository unit. That's where tools such as Watson can play a critical role."

The complexity of health care is such that relying on hard-and-fast rules works some of the time but certainly not in all cases. Thus, a computer that follows and understands rules—such as engineering computing—is insufficient to do advanced diagnostic work in health care.

"Lots of times the rules don't apply to our patients," says Grundy. "That's why we need computing power that is cognitive, that learns, that thinks and understands the human dilemma in a different way than a machine that is good at applying rules.

"The human brain can make a mistake up to 40 percent of the time. If you ask a question, the brain sometimes doesn't go back far enough. It makes assumptions that you are on the right path. It looks for those certifying bits of information our brain already reached. Watson is designed *not* to do that. Watson goes back and looks at *everything* with zero preconceived assumptions."

One small example suggests Watson's potential. At a large health plan, when someone calls for preapproval for a certain procedure the request goes to a nurse, where the correct decision is made more than 80 percent of the time. An experiment having Watson take over shows the computer making the correct call 99.9 percent of the time—and almost instantly.

From the most powerful computer ever built to smart phones carried by billions of humans, the potential of technology in health care is immense. A November 4, 2013, study in *Health Affairs* titled "The Impact of Health Information Technology and e-Health on the Future Demand for Physician Services" reports that "Health information technology and electronic health applications will likely change the shape of the health care workforce, by raising efficiency; allowing more patient care to be provided by physician assistants and nurse practitioners, and by generalist rather than specialist physicians; and by increasing the opportunity for patients to receive care remotely."

When the Christine Sinskys, Tom Bodenheimers, Gary Kaplans, Andrew Morris-Singers, Peter Pronovosts, Howard Brodys, Christine Cassels, and Paul Grundys of the world stand up together and work toward innovations that are not only patient-focused but also increase the level of satisfaction that physicians enjoy in their practice, something great and powerful is happening. When organizations such as the Centers for Medicare and Medicaid Services, ABIM, and dozens of professional associations stand up and work together to eliminate waste, improve quality, and control costs, something great is happening. These individuals and organizations represent thousands of health care innovators throughout the nation.

But the reality is that we need tens of thousands and then hundreds of thousands more like them. Their brand of patient-centered activism is happening at all levels, and this is what makes the Learning Coalition—as loosely formed as it may be—such a powerful force. Christine, Tom, Andrew, Peter, Gary, Howard, Paul, and all of their colleagues are active, contributing members of the Learning Coalition. They are making a difference in the lives of patients and doctors. And it is a beautiful thing to see.

9

Learning Coalition

The Pathway Forward

We absolutely have to make sure the gaps in your care are filled by the time you leave the office.

In fall of 2002, three Kaiser Permanente (KP) physicians from southern California gathered around a table at Paul's Cafe on Ventura Boulevard in Tarzana, California. Drs. Paul Minardi, Jeff Weisz, and Mike Kanter were dreaming about whether it might be possible to make a significant leap forward in caring for their patients.

As they talked, they made some notes on a napkin. "One of the things we had been able to do—but with variability—was connect patients to the preventive measures they needed," says Minardi. "In other words, to eliminate care gaps. The question was whether it might be possible to identify care gaps and preventive measures patients needed that would allow us to fill those needs at each and every touch point in our organization."

Could they set up a system to fill any patient-care gap—for a mammogram, blood work, colonoscopy, anything—whenever the patient touched KP in any way, at any level? Could they do it for every patient, every time, everywhere? This was the Holy Grail of patient care, in a sense. Historically, huge numbers of patients have gone about their daily lives in a potentially unsafe state—that is, without the benefit of known preventive measures that improve their health and save their lives. These care gaps were as dangerous as they were ubiquitous.

"We tossed around the concept of how to make as much of the care automated and systematized as possible, rather than relying on each individual doctor to remember to do every single thing that needed to be done," says Kanter. "That approach is not reliable or sustainable."

All three physicians felt a certain frustration knowing that so many patients were not getting the care they needed. As chief of the Department of Family Medicine and assistant medical director for the KP Riverside, California, region, Minardi oversaw population care management—caring for hundreds of thousands of patients with a variety of disease states.

"We really had to understand the care gaps," Minardi said. "The question for us was how do we get our great integrated care delivery system embedded into the practice of medicine in a timely and efficacious way so regardless of where a patient is seen we can care for them in a much more meaningful way."

The conversation was long and animated, and the three doctors left the café feeling a sense of excitement at the prospect of trying to put together such a system.

"We were dedicated to one thing and one thing only, and that is *patient first*," said Minardi. "This was in Riverside, where there was a history of innovation and some of the highest-quality rankings in KP. As physicians, we felt a sense of esprit de corps—that I belong to something bigger than myself."

By the early winter of 2003 Minardi, Weisz, and Kanter were at work on their idea, but the beginnings of the program—dubbed the Proactive Office Encounter—were humble.

"Our focus was on how to create systems of care and reliable approaches to care that we can replicate over and over and over again flawlessly at every point of care," Minardi said. "My frustration at the time was how do we do that given our antiquated systems and thousands of appointments per month? How do we do this in a systematic way so we can really touch every life?"

In the summer of 2003 Minardi had postcards sent to patients due or overdue for adult immunizations such as tetanus, diphtheria, and pneumococcal vaccine, and when the patient responded the order would be waiting.

Initially, the program remained very low-tech. A nurse would scan the list of upcoming patients for a day and note the preventive and other treatments for which they were due. That list would go to the primary care physician seeing the patient, and the doctor—with support staff—would work to fill the gaps. "It was a very clunky way for us to start," said Minardi, "but it was incredibly great because we were filling so many gaps."

By 2006 the entire program had been shifted from paper to the electronic health records (EHRs) within the vast KP system. This was akin to upgrading from a Model T to a Corvette. A patient who might need labs done or might need a pap smear or a mammogram, for example, would be identified in the EHR prior to the visit. A nurse would then create pending orders for all the testing, allowing the physician to review and execute the orders with a single click of a mouse.

"Everything matters," Minardi notes. "Everything counts. We have created the capacity to do all of the work necessary for the patient that eliminates the waste of a second or third visit."

With its system-wide EHR, KP built a rich store of data. "We would measure outcome metrics, immunization rates, hypertension control rates, and much more," says Minardi:

> We were constantly mining the data on our EHR asking questions: How many of our cardiovascular patients are on lipid agents, for example? We looked at all the HEDIS measures and our own clinical strategic goals for the year.
>
> If a patient shows up in the clinic and has not had a colorectal cancer screen test, diabetes test, or flu vaccine, we can identify that immediately upon your arrival and have your lab tests arranged right then. We absolutely have to make sure the gaps in your care are filled by the time you leave the office. You could show up for an allergy evaluation and wind up having a mammogram, or medicine readjusted for diabetes, or any number of things. We have identified your personal care needs and whether you show up in the pharmacy, interact with kp.org, call our phone line—any touch anywhere in KP—we will identify and deliver the care you need.
>
> *She said, "I'm not going to let you get out of here until you make your appointment."*

Rarely now do KP physicians find patients with late-stage breast or colorectal cancer. Think about that. The Proactive

Office Encounter approach prevents these diseases from reaching a stage where they can end a patient's life!

In a March 2009 KP case study, an internal KP analysis found that "along with other concurrent improvement initiatives, the Proactive Office Encounter has contributed to a 30 percent increase in colon cancer screenings, an 11 percent increase in breast cancer screening, a five percent increase in cervical cancer screening, and a 13 percent improvement in cholesterol control. If the program continues to advance at its current rate, it is projected that more than 10,000 lives will be saved per decade."

Minardi notes that "88 percent of our hypertensive patients are in control, and that is world class. It not only decreases horrible outcomes of hypertension, stroke, heart attack, renal failure, and vascular disease, it also minimizes and decreases the prevalence of all of those conditions as the hypertension is controlled and the care needs of those patients on the institution diminish significantly. Complications for these patients, such as headache or vision changes that would drive these patients in are not doing so, which has created huge value for both patients and the organization. It minimizes demand for services while improving patient outcomes."

A crucial element of the Proactive Office Encounter is that it is in place in all specialty clinics. Some work traditionally done in primary care was moved to where the patient happened to be. This provides better care overall and improves alignment between primary care and specialty care. It also means that all physicians and their teams work toward common goals that increases a sense of camaraderie and teamwork rather than each doctor or specialty working within a silo.

Perhaps the best way to illustrate the power of the Proactive Office Encounter is with the story of KP member Mary Gonzales. When Mary checked in for her appointment at Baldwin Park in the central San Gabriel Valley region of Los Angeles County, the EHR showed that she was due for a mammogram. Clinic receptionist Susan Salas noticed this on Mary's record and offered to schedule the mammogram for her. No, Mary said, she would schedule it for later on. She had scheduled mammogram appointments in the past and had to cancel them, but she told Susan that she would get around to it.

But Susan didn't budge. Says Mary, "She said, 'I'm not going to let you get out of here until you make your appointment.'"

In fact, Susan said she could get Mary in for the mammogram *that day*. Mary agreed. Her test that day and a subsequent biopsy revealed an aggressive tumor that was soon removed. Without the system that Minardi, Weisz, and Kanter envisioned and built—and without Susan's insistence—Mary says that she probably would have waited to have her mammogram. By then, she says, perhaps it would have been "too late."

This scenario was exactly what Minardi, Weisz, and Kanter were dreaming about back when they gathered around that table in Paul's Cafe on Ventura Boulevard in 2002. To say that these three dedicated physicians wanted to fill "all the care gaps" is accurate but sounds a bit clinical. What they really wanted to do was save Mary's life.

WORLD-CLASS OUTCOMES

We believe based on anecdotal evidence—talking with scores of doctors—that the Proactive Office Encounter has also helped to preserve and enhance physician careers at KP.

"Outside KP, there is bureaucracy beyond the pale," says Minardi. "Doctors have insurance companies in their face trying to chew them down on rates. Bureaucrats are all over them, Medicare is cutting their reimbursement, hospitals are after them to create greater revenue for them, and trial attorneys are after them like there is no tomorrow, and there are more mandates than ever before. Put it all together, and it is not a rosy picture."

At KP, while it is certainly not perfect, the lives of physicians are much more rewarding than in other systems. Minardi asserts "At KP we do an outstanding job of creating an environment where physicians' only focus is the patient and their needs as well as their family's needs. It helps us to be a vital business and, at the same time, put patients first. We leverage the group practice of medicine to ensure our patients' vitality and our financial vitality."

When KP achieves advances systemically, such as the Proactive Office Encounter, clinicians at other organizations often say that *we would like to be able to do that, but we're not KP.* But the reality is that KP couldn't do it until we did it in the southern California region. At KP, preservation and enhancement of career at a practical level means providing physicians with the team and resources they need to deliver the best possible patient-centered care. This means that any work that can be done by some other members of the care team preserves physician time and energy for patients.

"The basic things that happen in a practice and are a problem in other places are well controlled at KP, so the hassle factor to practice medicine here is mitigated," says Minardi.

One of the strengths of KP is that when strong leaders move on, they are replaced by other strong leaders.

When Dr. Weisz moved from southern California to the KP Northwest region, he was succeeded in southern California by Dr. Ed Ellison, who has continued the level of excellence in that area, building upon the culture of innovation and learning. Ellison is guided by a great mantra, borrowed from Cincinnati Children's: *to be the best at getting better.*

KP's relentlessly patient-focused work has produced dramatic results in a variety of areas. A look at multiple HEDIS measures for 2012 reveals that a variety of KP regions ranked first in the nation for

- Cholesterol management CAD—LDL screening,
- Cholesterol management CAD—LDL level <100,
- Comprehensive diabetes care—HbA1c testing,
- Comprehensive diabetes care—LDL level <100,
- Comprehensive diabetes care—medical attention for nephropathy,
- Comprehensive diabetes care—blood pressure control (<140/80),
- Breast cancer screening,
- Chlamydia screening in women (ages 16–20, 21–24, and total),
- Avoidance of antibiotic treatment in adults with acute bronchitis, and
- Antidepressant medication management—effective acute phase and effective continuation phase.

Innovation is built into the culture of KP. The Proactive Office Encounter work that originated in southern California has spread throughout KP. The same is true of outstanding work done in the northern California region, an area with dynamic innovators throughout. A couple of examples tell a powerful story.

In 2003 KP launched an innovative program to reduce heart attacks and strokes among members with heart disease and diabetes. It was dubbed the ALL program: Aspirin, Lovastatin, and Lisinopril. Aspirin helped thin the blood, Lovastatin is an anticholesterol medication, and Lisinopril helps control high blood pressure.

Within a year, the ALL program grew into the ALL/PHASE program: Preventing Heart Attacks and Strokes Everyday (PHASE). In addition to the three medications from the ALL program, the new elements added included efforts aimed at smoking cessation and increased exercise. Also, a beta blocker was added to protect patients from a second heart attack.

The ALL program produced dramatic results, reducing the rate of heart attack and stroke in high-risk populations by 60 percent among KP members. Similar to the Proactive Office Encounter, this is lifesaving work—and not just for KP members. In recent years, KP teams have shared the ALL/PHASE program with scores of safety net providers in communities that KP serves. In some cases, KP has provided the funding needed to implement the program in underserved areas. To date, more than thirty-five thousand patients at fifty-five safety net sites have joined the program.

Teams in northern California made similarly impressive progress on sepsis, one of the most dangerous threats to hospitalized patients. As often happens within KP, the sepsis innovation started on a small scale with a playbook to attack sepsis tested in two sites. It worked so well that it was spread rapidly throughout northern California and then to other KP regions.

"The first step in treating any medical problem is making the right diagnosis," observes Dr. Robert Pearl, CEO of The Permanente Medical Group. "In the case of sepsis, excessive deaths don't result from a lack of knowledge or from poorly trained doctors. They result from outdated approaches and cultural values left over from a different time in American medicine."

The KP teams have demonstrated an impressive ability to get far beyond those outdated approaches and cultural values and take on sepsis in a particularly effective manner. The initiative, reported in the *Joint Commission Journal* in November 2011 by a KP team led by Dr. Alan Whippy and titled "Collaborative Improvement in Sepsis Identification and Treatment—Kaiser Permanente's Performance Improvement System, Part 3: Multisite Improvements in Care for Patients with Sepsis," resulted in an increase in sepsis diagnosis per one thousand patients from "35.7 in July 2009 to 119.4 in May 2011. The percent of admitted patients who have blood cultures drawn who also have a serum lactate level drawn increased from a baseline of 27% to 97% in May 2011." The article concluded that "twenty-one cross-functional frontline teams redesigned processes of care to provide regionally standardized, evidence-based treatment algorithms for sepsis, substantially increasing the identification and risk stratification of patients with suspected sepsis and the provision of a sepsis care bundle."

HEALTHPARTNERS: THE DRIVE
TO ELIMINATE DISPARITIES

Another learning organization is HealthPartners, based in Minnesota. HealthPartners physicians reach beyond the day-to-day work of the clinic, taking responsibility for broader issues such as access for all members of the communities they serve. HealthPartners embodies a culture where many physicians act as healers-leaders-partners.

This approach is found in the work that the Health-Partners teams have done on disparities, led by Dr. Beth Averbeck, associate medical director for primary care. Averbeck and her colleagues have long been aware of significant gaps in care nationally: that whites are more likely to have preventive services than patients of color, that African Americans are as much as 2.2 times more likely to develop diabetes than whites, that American Indians have 2.8 times the prevalence of diabetes than the population average, and that Hispanics and Latinos are more than 1.5 times more likely to develop diabetes than whites.

Recognizing that in HealthPartners' home state of Minnesota demographic trends indicate that communities of color will grow faster than the white population up through at least 2025, Averbeck and her colleagues have been working on the disparities issue for more than a decade. As early as 2001, HealthPartners set up a cross-cultural task force in response to the Institute of Medicine aims defined in *Crossing the Quality Chasm*, which include equitable care.

HealthPartners was one of the first medical groups (starting in 2004) to collect demographic data from patients, including preferred language and self-identified race. This enabled HealthPartners teams to identify gaps and test strategies to reduce those gaps. By 2006 Health-Partners had sufficient data to segment results by specific populations, focusing on disparities in communities of color and disparities based on socioeconomic factors. Analyzing the data, Averbeck and her colleagues built strategies for improvement and in 2010 established specific aims to reduce racial and financial class disparities in health.

"Having information in the electronic health record indicating the patient's preferred language and self-identified race has allowed us to see how clearly we are no longer dealing with a homogeneous Scandinavian population," says Averbeck. "For example, Minnesota has the largest Somali population outside Somalia."

In the course of their work, Averbeck and her colleagues have come to shift their goal from cultural *competency* to cultural *humility*. "Cultural competency assumes we can know, while cultural humility says we're trying to learn and understand different cultures," says Averbeck.

Averbeck and her colleagues gathered teams of Health-Partners physicians and other clinicians as well as members of the community to identify barriers to care and find ways around them. One of the barriers was transportation, which HealthPartners solved by issuing vouchers to patients due for preventive screenings. Same-day mammograms required having mammography capability onsite in clinics. There was a significant fear among many people from Somalia that immunizations caused autism. With conversations that included a Somali medical student and a variety of men and women from the Somali community, HealthPartners physicians provided information on the safety and benefits of immunizations.

"There was concern among some Somali women about whether the gowns for mammography screenings were clean," says Averbeck. "We would never have known this was a concern unless we had asked and included them in conversations."

HealthPartners' commitment to decreasing disparities extended to incorporating compensation incentives for managers and physicians based on reducing disparities. HealthPartners' relentless commitment to the work "decreased the care gap around mammography rates between whites and nonwhites, a medical group goal," says Averbeck.

Different clinics tried different approaches to closing care gaps on a variety of tests and screenings, and "as soon as we found something that worked, we spread it. We went from two to six to all clinics—our usual mode of spread. We would try something in two clinics for a couple of months until there was a steady state, and then we spread it."

Examples of the progress include:

- Breast cancer screening. The gap between white patients and patients of color reduced from 8.2 percent in 2008 to 2.4 percent in 2013. Also, screening results for white patients and patients of color are above the HEDIS 90th percentile for all patients.
- Colorectal cancer screening. The gap between white patients and patients of color reduced from 26.2 percent in 2009 to 11.2 percent in 2013. HealthPartners starts colorectal cancer screening at age 45 for Native American and African American patients (per the Institute for Clinical Systems Improvement's "Health Care Guidelines: Colorectal Cancer Screening").
- Diabetes patient outcomes. The optimal diabetes rate for patients of color increased from 14 percent in 2007 to 40 percent in 2013.
- Diabetes patient outcomes. "Hemoglobin Alc tested within twelve months": 98 percent for whites, 96 percent for patients of color. "LDL tested within 12 months": 92 percent for whites, 91 percent for patients of color.
- Goals for LDL measurement. BP measurement: Goals and results for cholesterol (LDL) measurement and blood pressure measurement are above

the HEDIS 90th percentile for white patients and patients of color. (Source: HealthPartners)

LEARNING COALITION IN ACTION: THE POWER OF TRANSPARENCY

In the modern health care world, one of the most powerful patient-centered elements is transparency. A story from Cincinnati Children's Hospital Medical Center demonstrates the power of transparency to foster improvement in a lifesaving way.

In 2001 a shock reverberated throughout Cincinnati Children's when staff faced up to the reality that the hospital's care for children with cystic fibrosis (CF)—then considered among the best anywhere—was in fact *below* the national average.

Patients and their families, however, were in the dark. They did not know this because the Cystic Fibrosis Association did not publish the quality rankings of the nation's 117 CF hospital programs. The association told individual hospitals where they ranked but nothing more. And the teams at Cincinnati Children's had never revealed it.

But in the early 2000s, with courageous leadership determined to improve quality throughout the medical center, the Cincinnati Children's CF team decided that it had an obligation to disclose the truth to their patients and families. This would be painful. CF is a relentless disease that attacks the lungs of young patients, and while there is no cure, there are methods of treatment that can extend the lives of patients by years, sometimes many years. Still, the median life expectancy for a CF patient in the United States is only thirty-seven to thirty-eight years old.

Because CF patients require so much treatment, clinicians and their patients and families come to know one another very well over time, and strong personal bonds are often created between caregivers and families. Thus, there was anxiety among doctors, nurses, administrators, and board members who gathered the patients and families together one evening to reveal Cincinnati Children's disappointing national ranking.

The CF center leaders explained that they felt they owed this information to the families and said they would understand if any of the families sought care elsewhere. But the Cincinnati Children's team members also promised the families that they would go out and find the hospital with the very best care for CF in the country and would learn from the best, and then they would bring those best practices back to Cincinnati Children's and improve the care.

"Some of the family members were upset," recalls Dr. Jim Acton, then the CF center director (and currently chief of the Division of Pulmonary Medicine and Allergy at the University of Missouri Children's Hospital in Columbia). "They were not upset with our CF team. But this is a progressive disease, and it is important to stay on top of care and minimize progression, because you cannot undo permanent damage. So some of the reaction from parents was 'you mean my child may not be doing as well as he could be doing? How do we fix this?' We didn't go into the meeting with data that was just bad news. Sharing suboptimal outcome data is just bad news unless you come with a plan to make it better. So we shared the data along with a plan to work with them and include them in the process to make the numbers better." (Fortuitously, around this time Cincinnati Children's was awarded a Pursuing Perfection grant administered by the Centers for Medicare and Medicaid Services and funded by the Robert Wood Johnson Foundation. Cincinnati Children's used the grant to work on improving CF care.)

Parents provided valuable feedback. One mother told the care team that "'When I leave the vet with my dog I have a very clear plan of what to do with my dog when I get home,'" recalls Jeanne Weiland, nurse practitioner and CF clinic coordinator. "'But I leave the CF clinic and I have no idea what I am supposed to do at home with my daughter.'"

The Cystic Fibrosis Foundation was initially reluctant to provide the Cincinnati Children's team with the names of high-performing centers. The foundation's position was that the data was confidential. But when Don Berwick intervened on behalf of Cincinnati Children's and made the case that it needed the information to provide better care to its patients, the foundation relented.

"The CF Foundation gave us the names of five high-performing centers," says Acton. "We had conference calls with the center directors and subsequently met face-to-face during a CF conference with four of the five at the end of 2002."

Acton and his colleagues identified the University of Minnesota CF program as the place they most wanted to go and learn from, and they did so in the summer of 2003. It was not as though the University of Minnesota offered a silver bullet for CF care. No such thing exists. But the Cincinnati Children's team members learned key lessons that they brought back and applied in their center right away. They learned, for example, that the Minnesota team had an aggressive manner for managing newly diagnosed patients—a significant improvement over what was happening at Cincinnati Children's.

A particularly useful discovery came when the Cincinnati team joined the Minnesota group at its weekly meeting. "In Cincinnati, this meeting was focused on what had happened in clinic the prior week," says Acton. In Minnesota, they used the meeting to prepare the team for patients—a huge difference.

The Cincinnati team also learned that the Minnesota CF center was highly proactive about acting quickly on any changes in key metrics, even minor ones. "We learned that having timely access to our individual patient's clinical data and using it in a proactive manner is very important," says Acton. "Knowing our patient's clinical status and their trend and then using that information to be prepared for the clinic visit made clear what we needed to do with each patient."

The tendency in Cincinnati, according to Acton, was that if a patient's numbers were down in a certain area, there would be no treatment change. But in Minnesota when metrics shifted even slightly—measurements such as lung function or BMI (the main indicator of nutritional status in CF patients)—the care teams would immediately commence more aggressive treatment. "We set a lower threshold for intervention with quicker follow-up," says Acton.

The Cincinnati team also saw that the University of Minnesota clinicians engaged "on a different level" with patients and families, says Acton. "They did very well in the education and training with patients and families with mechanical airway clearance. They were very rigorous about making sure patients and families knew the most effective technique and that they were doing it correctly." The Minnesota team "had consistent focus on airway clearance in every visit as well as a heavy focus on early diagnosis," says Weiland. "With newly diagnosed patients, they had a very strong education program right from the start."

In the years since the disclosure of results to patients and families and the learning trip to the University of Minnesota, Cincinnati Children's CF results have markedly improved. Five key metrics that the Cincinnati team targeted have been transformed: improved nutrition and pulmonary function tests at home, reduced in-patient stays, an increase in flu vaccine rates, and greater community involvement.

"Our nutritional BMI improvement has increased by 15 to 20 percent, and the lung function of our patients is close to best in class," says Weiland. "Over time the culture has changed so that we track outcomes in real time and standardize care. We now have a much more standardized approach."

LEARNING FROM THE HIGHEST
(AND LOWEST) PERFORMERS

It is difficult to overstate the power of transparency as a means to improving quality in health care. Atrius Health is a sprawling Boston-area physician group with more than one thousand doctors spread over forty communities in eastern and central Massachusetts, together with a home health agency and a hospice. For many years, Atrius Health physicians were working under a variety of global contracts whose purpose was to pay Atrius for keeping its patients healthy. These contracts offered Atrius Health the opportunity to take financial risk for the care of its patients, whether that care was provided by Atrius Health clinicians, other specialists, hospitals, skilled nursing facilities, or pharmacies. Frequently there was a Pay-for-Performance (P4P) component that linked some limited quality measures to a bonus as well. In 2009 Blue Cross Blue Shield of Massachusetts offered a new Alternative Quality Contract (AQC) with a longer term and a much more extensive set of quality measures with the goal of paying provider organizations to keep patients as healthy as possible at the lowest possible cost. The concept was that by steering providers away from the inherent fee-for-service contracts whereby the incentive was to do more tests and procedures, the health of the Blue Cross member might improve even as the cost of his or her care would come down.

The contract was well designed to avoid withholding treatment from patients. More than two dozen specific quality metrics—a mixture between process and outcome measures—were targeted by Blue Cross. Provider organizations such as Atrius Health could earn additional payment by scoring high on these metrics. The Atrius Health physicians liked the contract because it aligned with their desire to improve the health of the population using the resources that they thought would best accomplish this objective.

It was not long before Drs. Richard Lopez, chief medical officer, and Dr. Kate Koplan, medical director for quality and performance improvement, discovered that while some Atrius sites performed at very high levels on some metrics, other sites performed at very low levels. Koplan convened monthly meetings, with the support of Lopez and Harvard Vanguard Medical Associates' director of internal medicine Dr. Karen Dasilva, for providers and leaders from across more than twenty Atrius sites (and groups throughout their system) to focus on a single metric. For example, they studied LDL cholesterol control one month and effective control of hypertension the next. What was unusual about these meetings was that Lopez and Koplan asked the two highest performers as well as the two lowest performers on these metrics to present their work.

During these monthly meetings, there was a brief review of the clinical literature supporting the health benefits of the particular quality metric. Then high and low performers would make a brief presentation focused on whether they had been paying attention to the metric in question, whether they had a particular structure in place to improve the metric, what barriers they faced, what successes they had (if any), and what their plan was going forward.

With more than fifty physicians and other clinicians and administrators sitting in a large meeting room, this was not always easy for the low performers. They knew that every other clinical team in the room was performing better than they were on the metric in question. But the physicians and other staff embraced the notion that going through this exercise promoted significant learning and was a way to directly and quickly improve quality care for their patients.

"The whole idea was to have a session on nonjudgmental data sharing that was focused on patient care," says Koplan, who has since moved on to Atlanta, where she now serves as associate medical director of quality and patient safety for The Southeast Permanente Medical Group in Georgia. "And there was a lot of trust among the groups, but even with that the low performers would get up in front of the group and say they were embarrassed—that it was difficult to stand up there and report their poor results."

Koplan went on to say that "Some high performers would get up there and basically say 'we don't know why we are good at this,' and we would probe and try and get at what exactly their approach was. Some low performers would say 'we know we are low because we are not paying attention to this,' while others would say 'we don't know why we're low.'"

This is work that goes to the core of the Learning Coalition culture. It requires awareness, humility, and courage as well as a determination to do what is best for patients. Critical lessons for improvement were presented at each meeting—not just for the lowest performers but for everyone. Over time, the power of this approach helped improve the group's performance on a wide variety of critical metrics.

Koplan emphasizes that improvement efforts at Atrius Health came in a variety of shapes and sizes—department meetings, site meetings, and much more. But she believes that these quality improvement meetings had a real impact. "The lower performers would say 'we do not want to be up here again,' and there were a few groups initially—during the first twelve to eighteen months—that were pretty consistently among the low performers in a number of areas of measurement," Koplan says. "But if you looked at them now, several years later, you would see that all of those groups had improved significantly, and some were among the top performers. Being at the bottom is a big instigator for action."

TOTAL HEALTH

Much of this chapter has focused on great work within clinics and hospitals, but the reality is that many determinants of health relate to lifestyle choices and environment. This is why the Learning Coalition throughout the nation is pushing so assertively to reach beyond the exam room and get to patients where they live and work.

It is our duty as healers-leaders-partners to reach into the community to improve the conditions—whatever they might be—that have an impact on the health of our patients. At KP, this means assuming broader responsibility for members' health, including nutrition, exercise, public education and safety, food supply, and a sustainable environment.

At KP, this is known as Total Health and is really the soul of KP. There is a profound commitment to Total Health from the medical group and throughout the health plan, and it derives from our founder, Dr. Sidney Garfield. In fact, it was Dr. Garfield who coined the term "Total Health." During the Great Depression, Dr. Garfield provided care to construction workers in the Mojave Desert. Part of his brilliance was creating a prepaid insurance plan whereby workers paid a nickel a day for coverage of all their health care needs. For Dr. Garfield, a major part of his work was going upstream to improve the overall health of workers—a truly pioneering approach to providing care.

The idea of Total Health has gone viral within KP, where the culture quickly embraced the ambition of engaging with patients on a wider variety of issues affecting health. Total Health has been at the top of the KP priority list for a decade. It was defined in 2003 as the KP "brand promise" and was defined in 2011 as KP's organizational vision: "To be a leader in Total Health by making lives better."

In 2004 KP launched its "Thrive" advertising campaign that brought the total health concept to life. "The 'Thrive' campaign was enormously resonant with consumers and members, and it triggered a broader thinking internally," says Christine Paige, senior vice president of marketing and digital services for KP. "We asked ourselves, what does it mean for our members to thrive? Are they thriving? What implications does that have for how we deliver care?"

"Total Health requires Kaiser Permanente to deploy all its assets," says Ray Baxter, PhD, senior vice president of community benefit, research, and health policy for KP, "from clinical care and prevention to research, from community health initiatives to shaping public policy. The Total Health portfolio includes focus areas, beginning with schools and workforce wellness; core clinical capabilities, such as the KP Integrated Care Model and proven behavior change strategies; and population strategies, such as Every Body Walk!, a comprehensive, national public awareness campaign aimed at getting people up and moving every day."

"To me," says Dr. Scott Young, "the *aha* moment here is that leaders in health care are recognizing that even if we make the health care system great, we could still lose the total health battle because of the prevalence of chronic disease, obesity, and lifestyle issues. You can have the highest-performing clinics and still lose at the end of the day. During our discussions, someone would say the key is income inequality, and someone else would say its about education, and another voice would say health depends on job security or the built environment, or nutrition, and it turns out everybody was right!"

Young and his colleagues believe that working with schools has the potential not only to help improve the health of students and teachers but also to possibly spread that impact to the families of students and teachers. "We believe we can affect the total health impact in schools promoting exercise and good wholesome foods," says Young. "So schools are one target for us. And we also recognize that our own workforce could be much healthier. It's one thing for us to tell others, but if we're not doing it ourselves with our own two hundred thousand employees, then it's a much harder sell."

Young goes on to say that "Healthy schools and a healthy workforce are the two big pieces. With the schools we have developed the program, and we are now forming partnerships and getting into the field. With the healthy workforce we are in the field now having employees take health-risk appraisals."

A key element in the internal effort among KP employees involves the commitment of the KP unions to the program. The relationship between KP management and its unions is one of the great strengths of KP. Union and management work together in an unusually close, harmonic relationship *for the benefit of the patient.*

John August, the retired executive director of the Coalition of Kaiser Permanente Unions, says that after a good deal of study he learned that many corporate wellness programs produce meager results. August and his colleagues believe that the problem is that in many wellness programs, incentives are based on an *individual's* performance. "You've got a carrot-and-stick approach to people who are not healthy, and while you might get some improvement, you are really neglecting the other 75 percent of the workforce that is in relatively good health," says August. "And that's where you see the slide."

Thus, KP is approaching workforce health quite differently. "Our program provides bonuses to the workforce when there is an achievement in *population* outcomes rather than individual outcomes," August says. "And the financial bonus is earned not by individuals but by an entire workforce in a region. We are looking for improvements in cholesterol, BMI, blood pressure, and smoking cessation across a group of employees. This is something I believe is revolutionary—rewards based on quality improvements for an entire population."

The partnership of management and unions at KP has proven effective through the years. "We've engaged in a very conscious transformation of roles of people at the front lines," says August. "Managers' roles must change from being a traditional supervisor to a leader and collaborator, and the union steward must change to become a leader and collaborator as well."

One of the most important steps KP has taken to help advance total health is to add physical activity to the list of vital signs monitored. Thus, in addition to such measurements as temperature, pulse, respiration, and blood pressure, KP physicians now list a measurement for exercise based on self-reporting from patients. Dr. Robert Sallis, a longtime KP family physician and developer of the Exercise Vital Sign (EVS), says, "There is no better indicator of a patient's health and longevity than the minutes per week of physical activity they engage in. The EVS is a great way to get the topic of exercise into the exam room and help initiate a discussion on how it can impact my patient's health." The very fact that it is defined as a vital sign gets patients' attention in a serious way.

"A huge improvement in physician communication with patients is that we can now link exercise and activity to medical and clinical outcomes," says Scott Young. "We can now say that people who exercise more are more likely to not have cancer, and if they do have cancer they are more likely to survive. We can say that people who exercise are more likely to not have diabetes and to avoid becoming obese."

KP is creating a new measure associated with prediabetes in an effort to identify members at risk for the disease. The goal is to prevent diabetes in members who have climbing BMI, blood pressure, or blood sugar—"a constellation of early warning signs," as Matt Stiefel, senior director at KP's Care Management Institute, puts it.

Lisa Schilling, vice president of national health care performance improvement for KP and director of the KP Performance Improvement Institute, offers an example. "We have about a half million patients with diabetes, but we have over 870,000 *at risk* for diabetes. And if we did nothing to prevent progression, in ten years we would double the number of patients with the disease," she says.

KP's powerful EHR system enables teams to identify members at risk for diabetes, cancer, cardiovascular disease, and more. And when these patients are identified by a primary care team, a team member contacts them and works with each individual on such things as physical activity, nutrition, stress management, and alcohol consumption.

"When we identify a person at risk, we have a conversation with them, and we connect them to resources that help with changes in lifestyle and behaviors," says Schilling. "This may involve a wellness coach or classes at the YMCA. When we explain to patients that certain behaviors can help them prevent disease, it gets their attention. They get the idea that with some lifestyle changes they can prevent the disease altogether."

The exploration of determinants of health is one of the most significant trends in health care today—and one of the fastest growing. Rarely in the past have physicians actively worked to impact how patients' health is affected outside the clinic. The antismoking initiatives of the 1970s and beyond are an example, of course. But more than ever, with the epidemics of chronic conditions, obesity, and unsustainable cost increases, our physicians must aspire to take on the role of healer-leader-partner.

Physicians must work to heal individual patients and must lead within health care organizations as well as more broadly and partner with other organizations—medical, civic, educational, and beyond—that have the power to impact the overall health of a community.

Research makes clear that diet, exercise, lifestyle, built environment, socioeconomic factors, race, genetics, and such are among the many determinants of health. Rather than relying only on clinical interventions, our doctors must be looking at the total health of the patient. Physicians can play broader roles as advocates, sponsors, and mentors in a variety of the areas that determine overall health. Increasingly in the years and decades to come, it will be healer-leader-partner physicians who have the greatest impact on the overall health of the population.

10

The Urgent Need
to Preserve and Enhance
Physician Careers

The best work anywhere should be the standard everywhere.

Harris Interactive, one of the leading research firms in the nation, has conducted an abundance of research in health care and reached a stark conclusion: "Any discussion with physicians must begin with acknowledging the degree to which fear of liability drives their decisions about diagnostic test and interventions. . . . They see tort reform as the elephant in the room that policy experts do not discuss."

The liability issue *is* the elephant in the room, and too often academics and policy experts fail to recognize this. It is one of the major underlying reasons why, as Harris Interactive has found, "the practice of medicine is . . . a minefield today. . . . Physicians today are very defensive—they feel under assault on all fronts."

Harris Interactive found that "the majority of physicians [54 percent] are pessimistic about the practice of medicine today." This is disturbing on many levels. When one considers the challenge ahead—achieving the Institute of Medicine's goals, reaching the Triple Aim, and implementing the Affordable Care Act—this level of pessimism is unsettling.

Transformational change in the U.S. health care system seems inevitable in the years to come, yet Harris Interactive found that "compliance with change depends on how much fight the docs have left in them. Some are still fired up to fight it, while others have already been beaten down."

This is as astonishing as it is alarming—the idea that some physicians may be too *beaten down* to lead us to a transformed health care system. This notion notwithstanding, an argument is often heard that the liability issue is exaggerated by physicians. When physician voices from the front lines of care are tuned out, as is sometimes the case, malpractice fears are dismissed. A lengthy indictment of physicians' malpractice concerns by Maggie Mahar in the HealthBeat Blog titled "Myths about Medical Malpractice: Part 2, Crisis or Hoax?" reported that "only" 42 percent of doctors are ever sued.

"Only" 42 percent? The article asserts that physicians' fears of litigation are "exaggerated." But when you dig a bit deeper into the issue—into what is on the minds of doctors—the fear of litigation is understandable and all too real.

The American Medical Association (AMA) reports that more than 60 percent of physicians over age fifty-five "have been sued at least once," according to an ABC television network report on the AMA study. The ABC report noted that "although most . . . claims are dropped or dismissed, the new survey from the AMA shows that most physicians will be sued for malpractice at some point in their careers" and that "the average defense costs between $22,000 for dropped or dismissed claims to more than $100,000 for cases that go to trial, according to data in the report from the Physician Insurers Association of America."

The liability crisis adversely influences the quality of patient care. When doctors overtreat as a defense mechanism—as a large percentage of physicians say they do—this is by definition less than ideal quality. Overtreatment impedes the flow of care, thus impacting access and resulting in a significant waste of dollars, as well as physician and support staff time in clinics and labs. The trauma of being accused of a harmful mistake is not fully appreciated outside the physician community. Doctors worry that if they make that one mistake—miss that one indicator or fail to order that one test—their professional lives could tumble down around them.

Part of our effort to preserve and enhance physician careers means joining together to solve the physician liability crisis. Many physicians and policy makers suggest that the answer is tort reform, and while reform of such laws deserves serious discussion, the liability crisis goes much deeper. Aaron E. Carroll, associate professor of pediatrics at Indiana University School of Medicine, has written insightfully about malpractice. He notes on his blog "The Incidental Economist" that a tiny minority of claims ever reach a courtroom. "The majority of claims [64 percent] are dropped, withdrawn, or dismissed," he wrote on April 16, 2012. Carroll writes that focusing on sensational tort claims "as a means to change the whole system (tort reform) doesn't always make a whole lot of sense."

If Carroll is correct—and we believe he is—then what should we focus on to solve the liability issue? The answer is clear: safety and transparency, which are essential elements of overall quality. Our approach to taking on the liability issue focuses first and foremost on making health care safer for all patients by spreading well-established best practices that significantly improve safety in hospitals and clinics. Second, our approach calls for following the recommendations of the Lucian Leape Institute at the National Patient Safety Foundation that calls for a series of steps, starting with transparency on any medical error.

We can create a much safer health care environment to reduce the overall threat of malpractice actions. Many outstanding facilities throughout the country have dramatically improved safety in their facilities. Among them is Virginia Mason Medical Center in Seattle, which adapted the Toyota Production System to health care more than a decade ago. This lean management approach has transformed Virginia Mason from the ground up, improving quality, safety, access, affordability, patient-centeredness, and efficiency—all the major measures.

The inspiration for the Virginia Mason safety methodology came directly from a Toyota factory floor. Dr. Gary Kaplan, the CEO of Virginia Mason, observed work on a Toyota assembly line. He and a number of his colleagues watched as a worker having trouble with a particular part pulled a cord that ground the entire assembly line to a halt. Supervisors rushed to the scene, collaborated with the worker, and quickly fixed the problem. Kaplan and his team learned that every worker on the line was empowered to stop the line to prevent a defect in a vehicle. Could a comparable system work within health care? Kaplan believed that it could. This would mean empowering every employee at Virginia Mason to pull the cord and stop the line (make a call or send a computer message) if there was any threat of harming any patient in any way. This Patient Safety Alert system has fundamentally changed the safety level at Virginia Mason.

"Patient safety is our foundation," says Cathie Furman, RN, Virginia Mason senior vice president of Quality and Compliance. "Our goal is zero defects, and all our efforts around safety are aimed at nothing less than that."

Virginia Mason has been recognized as one of the safest medical centers in the country. In 2012, HealthGrades, an online source for information about performance levels by physicians and hospitals, recognized Virginia Mason with a Patient Safety Excellence Award, and the Leapfrog Group, which conducts a highly respected national survey on the safety, efficiency, and quality of hospitals, gave Virginia Mason its highest safety rating.

Patient Safety Alerts quickly identify instances where a Virginia Mason team acknowledges an error, apologizes to the patient and the family, and assures the patient that no additional costs related to the mistake will be borne by the family.

In the years since the Patient Safety Alert system was put in place, Cathie Furman says that there is "a direct correlation between the number of [alerts] we have and our cost for liability insurance. As the number of alerts rises, the number of claims and lawsuits goes down."

Transparency is central to the Virginia Mason approach to safety and is also foundational to the approach from the Lucian Leape Institute. The institute was formed in 2007 by the National Patient Safety Foundation to provide both an overall vision and specific strategies to improve the safety of health care delivery. It is named for Dr. Lucian Leape, a Boston surgeon widely recognized as a leading expert on medical safety. Leape and his coauthors enunciated the basic approach to medical safety in a 2009 article titled "Transforming Healthcare: A Safety Imperative" in *Quality and Safety in Health Care*, a British medical journal:

> We envision a culture that is open, transparent, supportive and committed to learning; where doctors, nurses and all health workers treat each other and their patients competently and with respect; where the patient's interest is always paramount; and where patients and families are fully engaged in their care. In a learning organisation, every voice is heard and every worker is empowered to prevent system breakdowns and correct them when they occur.

Virginia Mason is a model for this approach. When a patient is harmed at Virginia Mason, doctors immediately disclose the error to the patient and the family. The physicians apologize for the mistake and explain precisely what went wrong. The doctors explain what is being done to make sure a similar error is never repeated on any future patient. Cathie Furman notes that the attending physician—not someone from risk management—meets with the family to offer an explanation and an apology. After a complete internal investigation, the physician will go back to the family with a more detailed explanation of what happened and exactly what the protocol will be to prevent such a mistake in the future.

According to the Leape Institute, "the free, uninhibited sharing of information . . . is probably the most important single attribute of a culture of safety. In complex, tightly coupled systems like healthcare, transparency is a precondition to safety. Its absence inhibits learning from mistakes, distorts collegiality and erodes patient trust." Other essential safety elements as stated by the Leape Institute include:

- Integrated care platforms;
- Consumer engagement, or "nothing about me without me";
- "Joy and meaning in work," suggesting that "care-givers cannot meet the challenge of making health-care safe unless they feel valued and find joy and meaning in their work"; and
- Restructuring of medical education "to reduce its almost exclusive focus on the acquisition of scientific and clinical facts and to emphasize the development of skills, behaviors and attitudes needed by practicing physicians. These include the ability to manage information; understanding of the basic concepts of human interaction, patient safety, healthcare quality and systems theory; and possession of management, communication and team-work skills."

PAYMENT REFORM

Just as liability is a serious issue facing physicians today, so too is how we pay for medical care in the United States. And on the payment front, encouraging work is being done by a variety of individuals and organizations.

We hold an innate bias concerning payment, of course, believing that the Kaiser Permanente prepayment method serves patients particularly well, and it is certainly one of the options that should be considered in the discussion going forward.

The Commonwealth Fund, a private foundation based in New York, is one of the most intellectually robust health care–related organizations in the United States. The fund supports excellent research on a wide variety of health care issues with an overall goal of promoting improved quality, access, and efficiency. Some of the foundation's best work has involved studying various ideas pertaining to payment reform. *Confronting Costs: Stabilizing U.S. Health Spending While Moving toward a High Performance Health Care System*, published in early 2013, is a good example. In this report, the Commonwealth Fund Commission on a High Performance Health System recommends

a set of synergistic provider payment reforms, consumer incentives, and system wide reforms to confront costs while improving health system performance. . . . Payment reforms would: provide incentives to innovate and participate in accountable care systems; strengthen primary care and patient-centered teams; and spread reforms across Medicare, Medicaid, and private insurers.

With better consumer information and incentives to choose wisely and lower provider administrative costs, incentives would be further aligned to improve population health at more affordable cost. Savings could be substantial for families, businesses, and government at all levels.

Another Commonwealth Fund report in August 2013 by Steve Guterman titled "Wielding the Carrot and the Stick: How to Move the U.S. Health Care System Away from Fee-for-Service Payment" noted that "not only does fee-for-service payment fail to provide incentives for efficiency, quality, or outcomes, it encourages the provision of unnecessary care and often discourages coordination of care and management of patients across providers and settings."

The call for a shift away from fee-for-service to payment for population health grows stronger each day. This approach is at the heart of the Alternative Quality Contract (ACC) created by Blue Cross Blue Shield of Massachusetts. Thus far, provider organizations working under the AQC report strong quality improvements. Whether the contract will prove to control costs over a sustained period of time is yet to be determined, but early indicators are promising.

A CEO Council report on payment reform in November 2012 titled "Remaking Health Care: Change the Way Providers Are Paid" echoes the call to shift away from fee-for-service to "explicitly gear our system around population health" and to "reshape financial incentives to meet the goal of population health, and build capacity and reimbursement systems to support it." The council calls for transparency as well as "uniform standards for health-care service quality, performance and price transparency so consumers can make value choices. And it should encourage states to follow suit." In a roundtable discussion about the report moderated by the *Wall Street Journal*'s Laura Landro, Mark Bertolini, CEO of Aetna, observed: "What happens in our system is if you get paid by a unit of service, you do more units of service. Our notion was to shift to population management. You assess the disease burden, the demography and the trends in the community and build a system and budget around that. You reward the system for improving the productivity and health of the population they serve."

Bertolini also invokes the transparency theme, calling for "a true market where people understand what the prices are for health care. Today, that's concealed. Imagine a supermarket where you go in with your cart and pull items off the shelf with no prices on them. You take it up to the counter. It's scanned. The clerk swipes your card and says, 'In thirty days you'll get your credit card bill, and you'll know how much your groceries cost.' Would you shop there? But that's how the health care system works. We need to create transparency in the system so people can understand how much health care costs."

One of the most powerful payment reform trends involves employers, especially large companies with significant market power, getting involved with the care of their employees—both its cost and quality—as never before.

Tom Emerick, coauthor with Al Lewis of *Cracking Health Costs,* has worked as a benefits consultant with some of the largest corporations in the country. Emerick predicts that we are "on the verge of a sea change in how employers pay for health care" and that employers are focused on moving toward paying for quality outcomes rather than procedures. Emerick says that the enormous cost burden on all corporations of employee health coverage has employers focused on benefits as never before. The old definition in the employer world was "is care delivered to a gold standard?" But Emerick says that major employers have a new definition: "First is the care needed and appropriate, then is it delivered to a gold standard?"

Having worked with many Fortune 500 employers, Emerick sees the Centers of Excellence model adopted by Walmart as an important future component of health benefits. The idea is to identify Centers of Excellence where the care is measurably excellent on quality and where price is competitive. Walmart has identified a number of such centers and will be sending tens of thousands of patients to these provider organizations in the years to come with the goal of better care at a lower cost. Emerick predicts that within no more than five years this will be the norm among Fortune 500 companies.

Paul Grundy has an interesting take on the payment reform issue, suggesting that we need "multiple dials," including a mixture of fee-for-service, capitated global payments, bundled payments, and more. "If you think about it that way and you are not afraid to put those dials in place, then you can adjust them based on what is working and what is not," says Grundy. "No matter how many dials you have, some will be gamed, and you have to have the ability to make adjustments."

The best work anywhere should be the standard everywhere.

Where does this leave us? There is so much good work being done in our country today—so many physicians who have stepped forward, worked cooperatively with others, and triggered breakthrough improvements—yet far too often these improvements fail to spread. And too many physicians are sitting on the sidelines, working in often dysfunctional organizations unable or unwilling to adopt some of the best that the Learning Coalition has to offer.

We do not minimize the challenge that spreading innovation presents. And we respect the notion that cultures are quite different in health care organizations and that adapting proven solutions often requires adjustments to fit comfortably into a particular local culture.

The aspiration to turn the best work *anywhere* into the standard *everywhere* still seems far away. Yet there is no doubt that the building blocks for a better future are out there. We see unmistakable signs of growing ranks of physicians who are adopting the healer-leader-partner approach. We see it from Christine Sinsky, Tom Bodenheimer, and their colleagues, who found not just an example or two but *twenty-three high-functioning primary care practices*. Their findings and recommendations, if spread throughout the country, could help transform primary care in our nation.

The grassroots initiative at Harvard Medical School to not only save but also greatly enhance the primary care program is encouraging, as is the healer-leader-partner approach by young physicians joining together with Andrew Morris-Singer in founding and expanding the group Primary Care Progress. National leadership by Paul Grundy and others who embody the concept of healer-leader-partner has provided inspiration and direction to thousands of physicians seeking to innovate on behalf of their patients.

And when we imagine physicians summoning their inner idealist and joining with others to dream of patient-care breakthroughs, we are captivated by the efforts of Paul Minardi, Jeff Weisz, and Mike Kanter as they brainstormed about how to better care for large populations of patients to eliminate perilous gaps in care. (We think they deserve a plaque at Paul's Cafe in Tarzana!)

Beth Averbeck and her colleagues at HealthPartners have recognized the power of physicians as healers-leaders-partners as they acknowledge their obligation to identify and eliminate significant racial disparities in care. Kate Koplan, Rick Lopez, and their colleagues at Atrius Health in Massachusetts have had the courage to explore and compare the highest and lowest performers on a variety of metrics—work that clearly subsumes physicians' egos and makes amply clear their deep commitment to the well-being of patients.

NEXT STEP: PHYSICIAN COMPACT

So the question is, what can we do to encourage more doctors to step forward as these physicians have done? We think that part of the answer might involve creating a new deal with doctors—a physician compact.

Physicians are at the heart of our health care system. The article by Rob Nesse, Gary Kaplan, and Jack Cochran asks, "Which stakeholder—physicians, hospitals, health plans, or others—will lead delivery system transformation? *We believe it must be physicians*. Among all providers, physicians have a disproportionate impact on the health care system, and therefore have a disproportionate opportunity and responsibility to lead change" (emphasis added). It is impossible to imagine solving the U.S. health care challenges of quality, safety, access, and affordability *without* physicians playing a leading role. "Physicians are ideally positioned, and in fact compelled, to take responsibility for helping shape the health care system—not just their own practice," the article states.

Jeff Weisz, one of the visionaries back at Paul's Cafe, made this observation in his book *It's a Great Time to Be a Physician*: "Sustainable healthcare systems can be built only if physicians lead the transformation, and if we are leaders in the teams and systems that deliver health care. This is really a change in our identity. We were trained to deliver health care not to lead."

Our nation urgently needs a unified effort by physicians to improve all aspects of health care. The foundational belief of this book is that fixing the physician crisis

is a prerequisite to achieving access, quality, and affordability throughout the United States.

Remember those five hundred frustrated physicians
interviewed during the Listening Tour in Colorado?
Regrettably, that is the current state of countless doctors
throughout the nation. And they need our help, just as
those physicians in Colorado needed help to be liberated
and supported to care for their patients. Doctors in our
nation need our support to preserve and enhance their
careers—*so they can do their best for patients.*

We need a new deal with physicians. Just as the doctors in Colorado needed preservation and enhancement
of careers to trigger a surge in the quality of patient care,
so too do we need a comparable deal now for the nation.
This work to preserve and enhance physician careers is
so critical that, as Bodenheimer says, "the Triple Aim
should be a quadruple aim, with clinician and staff satisfaction a necessity to achieve the other three aims."

Physician compacts are deals that health care organizations make with their doctors. More and more organizations throughout the country are turning to compacts
to make as explicit as possible what the organization can
expect from doctors and what doctors can expect from
the organization. In crass terms, the compacts are gives
and gets. *We the organization will do x; we the doctors will do
y.* (Compacts were originated by Jack Silversin of Amicus
Consulting in Cambridge, Massachusetts.)

OUR OBLIGATION TO PHYSICIANS

If we were to sketch a compact—an agreement between
physicians and *everyone else* (patients, hospitals, health
plans, employers, administrators, government, and other
clinicians)—what might it look like? As stakeholders in

the transformation of health care in the United States, we pledge to provide the essential elements that support physicians in their lifesaving work. Specifically, we pledge to work to

- Preserve and enhance physician careers,
- Support primary care by being sure the entire team takes responsibility for the work,
- Take on the liability crisis on behalf of all physicians in all specialties and improve safety of care to reduce the threat of malpractice actions against physicians, and
- Strengthen and expand the Learning Coalition.

Preservation and enhancement of physician careers was an important element that triggered the dramatic turnaround in quality as well as patient and provider satisfaction in Colorado. Preservation and enhancement means creating precisely the kind of systems that Sinsky, Bodenheimer, and others reported on that enable doctors to operate at the top of their license: to distribute work that can be done by others to others, to enable doctors to do what they are best at and trained for, and to do the work that brings physicians the greatest sense of professional satisfaction *and most benefits patients*. But there are also important benefits for physicians and other clinicians as well. Adopting innovative methods that exist today alleviates the unsustainable pressures that doctors face and enables primary care physicians to see all of their patients during the course of the day and complete all charting and other administrative work by early evening.

Here is what we do *not* mean by preservation and enhancement of physician careers. We do not mean returning to the good old days of physician pampering whereby doctors were autonomous and reluctant team players. It is in no way about doctors who feel victimized or entitled.

Support Primary Care

The building blocks that Bodenheimer and his colleagues identified from their study of primary care clinics are essential elements that improve the quality of care and the level of physician satisfaction. Is it too much to ask that these elements—listed above—be present in every clinic in our nation within a reasonable period of time?

The great majority of medical students are choosing to go into specialty fields that are more lucrative than primary care. This is why we should support students choosing primary care by providing substantial tuition support and loan relief. This will not only ease the burden on students but will also perhaps attract a greater number of students to select primary care.

This is in no way meant to underrate the immense importance of all of the medical and surgical specialties. Specialty care is crucial, yet experience globally indicates that higher-quality primary care leads to better care overall.

We must also take on the liability crisis to improve patient-care safety and reduce the threat of malpractice actions against physicians. The Harris Interactive analysis is instructive: "Any discussion with physicians must begin with acknowledging the degree to which fear of liability drives their decisions about diagnostic tests and interventions."

This is where the combination of profound safety improvement coupled with transparency can be a game changer. The powerful combination that we described above between the Virginia Mason Patient Safety Alert system along with the Lucian Leape Institute approach to dealing with errors can fundamentally change the nature of the liability threat to physicians.

Strengthen and Expand the Learning Coalition

The Learning Coalition aspires to become the "innovation accelerator" (in Arnie Milstein's words) that we need. There are many obstacles, but the most difficult and insidious is the large number of health care organizations that are, in the words of Maureen Bisognano, "hanging on, clinging to the status quo."

This approach is antithetical to the best interests of patients and providers. The reality is that the early adopters/innovators from the Learning Coalition have taken the risks and done the early work that shows a better way in dozens of areas within health care.

PHYSICIANS' OBLIGATIONS TO PATIENTS AND OTHER TEAM MEMBERS

In some ways, the other side of the compact—physicians' responsibilities to the patients and other team members—mirror our responsibilities to doctors. In return for the above, physicians agree to expand their horizons and recognize and acknowledge that the world is changing at a dizzying pace, and they also agree that physicians must change with it.

Physicians pledge to

- Become healers-leaders-partners and
- Become active members of the Learning Coalition.

Physicians have a disproportionate impact at the front lines of care and therefore must accept disproportionate responsibility and accountability. And when they commit to being healer-leader-partners and active Learning Coalition members, they are committing to providing better care for their patients. Physicians must accept a much broader role than ever before and engage on all issues that impact the health of their patients—whether those issues involve access, safety, quality, affordability, or anything else. It is essential that all physicians learn to become superb team members working collaboratively with *all* other care team members with a laser focus on what is best for the patient.

Join the Learning Coalition

Physicians as healer-leader-partners have a responsibility—to their colleagues and especially to their patients—to actively seek best practices and to bring those approaches home and apply them. Identifying proven practices in other organizations and applying them at the home organization to improve quality, safety, and efficiency is an effective way to shrink the chasm between the best performers in health care and the rest.

Berwick has noted that "It's not hard to describe the health care system we want; it's not even hard to find it. . . . Among the gems and the jewels throughout our country . . . lie answers; not theoretical ones, real ones, where we can go and visit these organizations and see how good they are."

Doctors have a responsibility to advocate for and lead the spread of best practices and to find innovations that impact patients and bring them home. If a physician group is having difficulty with flow in primary care, it is the doctor's job to find a place (or places) where the problem has been solved. Visit that facility, learn the solution, and bring it home. Physicians have a responsibility to know the best in any given area and to apply it in their own hospitals and clinics.

No health care organization holds a monopoly on best practices. Someone somewhere is doing something important in terms of care better than you are. We love the story of what Cincinnati Children's did to improve its cystic fibrosis program—that they identified the best and went there to learn. This search for the best should create a crisscross pattern throughout the country of provider organizations seeking out the very best performers in every area.

Here is where Arnie Milstein's analogy is so apt. As he puts it, "We need to shrink that gap between top performers and all the rest by a lot. Think about a race in the Olympics: the last sprinter in the 100-yard dash doesn't finish two or three seconds after the leader, he or she finishes two- to three-tenths of a second after the leader. All Olympic sprinters are excellent. That's what we need in medicine—everyone crossing the finish line on the heels of the winner."

Again where does this leave us? In a way, it brings us back to where we began, with physicians alleviating suffering, improving the quality of patients' lives, and even saving their lives.

If we are true to our mission to preserve and enhance physician careers so that they may provide the finest possible care, then we are drawn back to Antonio and his dad and to Lexi and Syd Stark and their parents.

Antonio and the Stark twins relied on physicians who were deeply engaged in and passionate about their work and considered it as much a calling as a profession.

Too often today, however, that is not the case for countless doctors. The doctor crisis is a complex variety of forces preventing physicians of all stripes from putting their patients first at every step in the care process—forces such as regulation, bureaucracy, and insurance company interference. (The beauty of KP is that the insurance company partners with KP physicians and hospitals in an integrated system, with the patient front and center.)

We believe that there is a clear pathway to a much improved health care system characterized by access, quality, and affordability, and we believe that this pathway runs directly through the Learning Coalition. Following that pathway requires cultural change. It requires shedding the fear that comes with asking hard questions about one's hospital or practice. It requires asking the question—about every area in your hospitals, clinics, and physician practices—of who is doing what you do *but better*. Who has a much lower rate of falls with injuries than you? A lower infection rate? A lower readmission rate? Which physician practices have the vast majority of their patients with diabetes under control on all key metrics? Which physician group has a much higher physician satisfaction rate than yours? How did they do it?

Is your organization as diligent about filling care gaps as Paul Minardi, Jeff Weisz, and Mike Kanter at Kaiser Permanente? If not, then some of your patients are going about their lives in an unsafe condition. How can you let that happen when you know that Minardi and his colleagues have a system to solve that problem?

Have you developed a marketplace of innovation/ ideas within your organization? Do you convene the highest and lowest performers on a variety of meaningful outcome measures to engage in learning, as Drs. Rick Lopez and Kate Koplan did at Atrius Health in Massachusetts? Are you engaged in "the free, uninhibited sharing of information" that the Leape Foundation says is essential for authentic transparency and safety?

What do you think patients want? Do they want a hospital or a doctor who not only isn't the best but also doesn't know who the best is? A hospital or doctor failing to look actively for other provider organizations from whom they can learn? Do patients want their providers to decide *not* to participate in the Learning Coalition?

If we are going to realize Arnie Milstein's vision of all "crossing the finish line on the heels of the winner," then health care must become a much stronger learning industry. This means that the Learning Coalition must be a marketplace where innovation and ideas are discussed and traded, where everyone teaches what they know best and everyone else learns, or as Maureen Bisognano puts it: "All teach, all learn."

Physicians as healer-leader-partner have a responsibility to their colleagues and especially to their patients to actively seek frontline best practices and to bring those approaches home and apply them. They have a responsibility to make clear that this work involves investments in physician leadership development and training that yield important dividends for patients.

Sinsky and Bodenheimer have identified twenty-three top performers in primary care. Have you sought to learn from any of them? Visited any of them? Is your answer—as is so often the case in health care—*I am too busy. We are too busy.*

Too busy is surrender to the status quo. Everyone in health care can legitimately make this claim, and yet tens of thousands of members of the Learning Coalition *make time* to go out and find ideas that improve care for their patients. Imagine saying to patients, yes, it is true we have dozens, scores, hundreds, or thousands of capable people working here in our organization, but we are unable to figure out how to spring some of these people free to scout out some of the best work in the country and bring it back so we can improve quality, safety, access, and affordability.

As a nation, as an industry, the only way we can achieve the goal of "the best work *anywhere* as the standard *everywhere*" is if provider organizations launch unending explorations for innovations and ideas—for work that is better than what they have and that will improve the quality of care.

The foundational belief of this book is that fixing the physician crisis is a prerequisite to achieving excellence in access, quality, and affordability throughout the United States, and it is impossible to imagine reaching this goal without physicians playing a leading role in making health care a far stronger learning industry than it is today. If more physicians take on the role of healer-leader-partner and actively engage with the Learning Coalition, there is no doubt that we can bring great joy to the practice of medicine—that we can enable physicians to have the resources and time they need to put patients first every time.

Acknowledgments

We owe a great debt to friends and colleagues at Kaiser Permanente, including Bernard Tyson, Dr. Scott Young, Dr. Amy Compton-Phillips, Chris Grant, Amy Lou, Robin Dilworth, Ilene Moore, Glen Hentges, Jean Sud, Maryam Malek, Alide Chase, George Halvorson, Ted Eytan, Lisa Schilling, Yan Chow, Diane Gage Lofgren, Holly Potter, Chris McCarthy, Christi Zuber, Estee Neuwirth, John August, and Jed Weissberg. Much gratitude goes to Dina Piccoli, who is a key leader and partner in our leadership training, and to Jenn Holguin, whose constant vigilance and patience keeps our work on track.

Nancy Taylor provided superb leadership through the process of writing the book, and Kim Corteen played a key role in making it all come together.

We are indebted to an outstanding group of colleagues and physician leaders from the Permanente Medical Groups, our executive medical directors: Drs. Nabil Chehade, Ron Copeland, Ed Ellison, Robert Pearl, Rob Schreiner, Mike Soman, Geoff Sewell, Jeff Weisz, and Bill Wright.

Thanks goes to Jim and Emily Stark for their generosity in sharing their extraordinary story and to Drs. Brad McDowell, Royal Gerow, Michael Handler, Joseph Janik, Peter Hulac, and Robert McDuffie, who put the plan together to separate the twins. We are grateful to the anesthesia team, which included Drs. Theresa Youtz and Patti Coughlin, who also played a central role.

We are grateful to inspirational leaders in health care from whom we have learned a great deal, including Paul O'Neill, Jim Anderson, Karen Ignani, and Maureen Bisognano and her team at IHI, including John Whittington and Tom Nolan. We are also grateful to the team at the Alliance of Community Health Plans, particularly Patricia Smith and Lynne Cuppernull, and to the American Medical Group Association and its CEO, Don Fisher.

We are also grateful to Len Nichols, Steve Shortell, Nicolaus Henke, Morten Hansen, Jeff Bliss, and Tanya Chermak.

We owe a great debt to numerous physician leaders throughout the United States, true healer-leader-partners including Drs. Don Berwick, Gary Kaplan, Lucian Leape, Arnie Milstein, Peter Pronovost, Paul Grundy, Howard Brody, Christine A. Sinsky, Tom Bodenheimer (and the entire Joy in Practice team), Rachel Willard, Uma Kotagal, Beth Averbeck, Gene Lindsey, Rob Nesse, Bob Mecklenburg, Elliott Fisher, Brian Rank, Chris Cassel, John Toussaint, and Andrew Morris-Singer.

Teachers and mentors on this journey include Dave Dibbell, Jeff Pfeffer, Merwyn Hayes, Amy Edmondson, and Dr. Charles A. Tracy.

At HealthPartners, we are grateful to Mary Brainerd, Beth Waterman, Nancy McClure, and Tessa Kerby. At Atrius Health, we owe a debt to Dr. Richard Lopez, Dr. Kate Koplan (who now serves as associate medical director of quality and patient safety for The Southeast Permanente Medical Group in Georgia), and Marci Sindell.

At PublicAffairs, we are grateful to Clive Priddle, Susan Weinberg, Peter Osnos, Lisa Kaufman, Melissa Raymond, and Jamie Leifer.

In Colorado, Drs. Bill Marsh, Patty Fahy, John Merenich, Andy Lum, Larry Hergott, Eric Christiansen, Berry Morton, Kim Adcock, Victor Collymore, Mike Chase, Jandell Allen-Davis, Andy Wiesenthal, Mark Wilson, and Scott Smith played important roles in our turnaround. The same is true for Dennis Helling, Linda Smith, Jill Bansek, Tracy Burke, and Debbie Jackson. Thanks also to Carol Mehlman, who has been available in supporting this book from the Denver work to current research.

To the five hundred KP physicians who shared their frustration, their thinking, and their wisdom on the Listening Tour of 1999, we are deeply grateful.

Notes

PREFACE

In the preface we rely on Dr. Jack Cochran's firsthand experiences as well as data provided by Harris Interactive, a New York–based research firm. We also rely on Jane Sarasohn-Kahn, "3 in 5 Physicians Would Quit Today If They Could," Health Care Blog, October 8, 2012, the healthcareblog.com/blog/2012/10/08/3-in-5-physicians -would-quit-today-if-they-could/. The blog entry was based on a survey by the Physicians Foundation. We rely as well on Liselotte N. Dyrbye and Tait D. Shanafelt, "Physician Burnout: A Potential Threat to Successful Health Care Reform," *JAMA* 305(1) (May 18, 2011): 2009–2010.

CHAPTER 1

In chapter 1, we rely on extensive coverage of the Stark family from several news sources and multiple articles from the *Denver Post,* including "Parents Pray for Health of Joined Twins," April 27, 2001, and "Parents of Conjoined Twins Opt for Separation Surgery," April 29, 2001, both by staff writer Allison Sherry.

We rely on Stephanie Riggs, "Connected for Life," *Colorado View Magazine,* Winter 2011; *CBS News 48 Hours,* February 11, 2009 (correspondent Jane Clayson); and an interview on CNN's *Larry King Live* with the Stark parents, October 4, 2002.

We rely as well on the case report of B. C. McDowell, B. E. Morton, J. S. Janik, R. K. Gerow, M. H. Handler, A. D. Lowenstein, J. H. Cochran, P. Coughlin, T. Youtz, and S. Conlan, "Separation of Conjoined Pygopagus Twins," *Plastic and Reconstructive Surgery: Journal of the American Society of Plastic Surgeons* 111(6) (May 2003): 1998–2002. The article does not identify the Stark girls as the subjects of the surgery, although physicians involved with the case made it clear that the article is drawn directly from the Stark case.

We also rely on recollections of the surgery from Dr. Brad McDowell.

CHAPTER 2

We rely on a presentation by Len Nichols at the Permanente Executive Leadership Summit, May 2012, Santa Barbara, California. We rely as well on Arnold Milstein and Steve Shortell, "Innovations in Care Delivery to Slow Growth of US Health Spending," *JAMA* 308(14) (October 10, 2012): 1439–1440.

We rely on Dr. Donald Berwick's Foreword to Charles Kenney's book *Transforming Health Care: Virginia Mason Medical Center's Pursuit of the Perfect Patient Experience* (Productivity Press, 2011).

CHAPTER 3

We rely on information from the Center for Shared Decision Making at Dartmouth-Hitchcock Hospital. We also rely on ideas expressed in various settings by Dr. Arnold

Milstein as well as Dr. Gene Lindsay, former CEO of Atrius Health in Massachusetts.

We rely on Jack Cochran, Gary Kaplan, and Rob Nesse, "Physician Leadership in Changing Times," *Journal of Delivery Science and Innovation,* forthcoming in the spring of 2014.

CHAPTER 4

Part II of the book (chapters 4–7) relies largely on Dr. Jack Cochran's personal experiences and recollections of events while he served at the Colorado Permanente Medical Group. In addition, we rely on interviews with Drs. Bill Wright and Bill Marsh.

CHAPTER 5

We rely on Drs. Bill Wright, Bill Marsh, John Merenich, Patty Fahy, and Jeffrey Pfeffer, professor at Stanford Business School.

CHAPTER 6

We rely on Drs. Bill Wright; Patty Fahy; Dennis Helling, executive director of Pharmacy Operations and Therapeutics for KP Colorado; and Linda Smith, senior director for Nursing Services and Quality for KP Colorado.

We rely as well on A. H. Rosenstein, "Original Research: Nurse-Physician Relationships: Impact on Nurse Satisfaction and Retention," *American Journal of Nursing* 102(6) (June 2002): 26–34.

The "Code of Conduct" discussed in chapter 6 is as follows:

Colorado Permanente Medical Group [CPMG] physicians demonstrate commitment to our patients, practices, and one another by providing high-quality, responsible medical care in a professional manner.

In meeting this commitment, CPMG physicians will:

1. Interact with other physicians, practitioners, and staff in their department, CPMG Leadership, and contacts in the community in a collegial, supportive, and professional manner.
   - Give feedback to colleagues in a professional manner.
   - Give corrective feedback to staff in a respectful manner away from patients and other staff.
   - Take concerns about a colleague which cannot be resolved directly to the department chief.
   - Express dissenting views in a respectful manner.
   - Accept responsibility and seek solutions to problems.
   - Give candid and timely feedback on peer/staff evaluations.
2. Provide excellent service to patients and internal customers:
   - Communicate patient care plans, consultations, and treatments back to referring providers.
   - Maintain strict patient confidentiality.
   - Treat members as valued customers.
   - Maintain appropriate provider-patient boundaries.

- Be punctual in all medical care settings (medical center, hospital, etc.).
- Maintain high-quality provider-patient relationships by any member satisfaction measurement (Art of Medicine, Patient Satisfaction, etc.).
- Attempt to resolve patient concerns.
- Assume responsibility in general for decreasing his or her patient waiting time for appointments when the wait is unacceptably prolonged.
- Respond appropriately to hospitals, page operators, and others.
- Be flexible in accommodating changes in patient demand to best meet the needs of the patient and the medical group.
- Balance multiple and at times unexpected or conflicting demands of patients.
- Clearly explain the plan for care to the patient to better ensure patient compliance and satisfaction.
- Demonstrate courtesy, respect, and a caring attitude to patients in order to enhance the provider-member relationship.
- Control emotional reactions toward patients and others.

3. Support the Principles of Medical Practice (Policy No. 5.03, Appendix A) and be careful stewards of our members' resources.
4. Participate as members of the health care team:
   - Meet work unit requirements and equitably share in the workload to ensure the department's needs are met.

- Participate in Quality Assurance activities and follow accepted clinical guidelines.
- Attend and participate in departmental meetings and team improvement activities.
- Schedule time-off requests in a fair and collaborative manner subject to department needs.
- Avoid maligning or undermining colleagues to patients or other physicians and staff, either verbally or in writing.
- The supervision of and collaboration with midlevel practitioners is strongly encouraged.

5. Contribute to the success of the Medical Group:
   - Be an advocate of Kaiser Permanente and its principles.
   - Follow the policies and directives of the Board of Directors and administration.
   - Support and participate in the development and implementation of strategic change initiatives.

[This Code of Conduct was not intended as an exhaustive statement about professional conduct and did not limit the discretion of Medical Group management in addressing concerns regarding conduct.]

CHAPTER 7

We rely on Drs. Bill Wright and Patty Fahy. In addition, we rely on Tracy Burke, project manager for Service Quality at KP Colorado, and Professor Amy Edmonson of the Harvard Business School for their particular insights concerning the Play to Win program.

CHAPTER 8

We rely on Christine A. Sinsky, Rachel Willard-Grace, Andrew M. Schutzbank, Thomas A. Sinsky, David Margolius, and Thomas Bodenheimer, "In Search of Joy in Practice: A Report of 23 High-Functioning Primary Care Practices," *Annals of Family Medicine* 11(3) (May–June 2013): 272–278. We also relied on work done by Dr. Tom Bodenheimer at the University of California San Francisco School of Medicine. We rely as well on Drs. Andrew Morris-Singer and Paul Grundy.

For Tom Bodenheimer's article about the power of primary care, see "Primary Care—Will It Survive?," *New England Journal of Medicine* 355 (August 31, 2006): 861–864, http://www.nejm.org/doi/full/10.1056/NEJMp068155.

For detailed descriptions of the building blocks given in Chapter 8, see Rachel Willard and Tom Bodenheimer, "The Building Blocks of High-Performing Primary Care: Lessons from the Field," California HealthCare Foundation, April 2012, http://www.chcf.org/~/media/MEDIA%20LIBRARY%20Files/PDF/B/PDF%20Building BlocksPrimaryCare.pdf, and "Profiles in Primary Care: Patient-Centered Medical Homes and the 10 Building Blocks of High-Performing Primary Care," 2012, http:// primarycareprogress.org/insight/4/profiles.

Here is a sample of some of the primary care clinics visited by the Sinsky team (with the number of physicians in each clinic in parentheses):

- Brigham and Women's Hospital in Boston (7)
- Cleveland Clinic in Strongsville, Ohio (103)

- Group Health in Olympia, Washington (36)
- Newport News, Virginia, Family Practice (5)
- ThedaCare in Oshkosh, Wisconsin (5)
- Southcentral Foundation in Anchorage, Alaska (115)
- Harvard Vanguard in Medford, Massachusetts (14)
- University of Utah in Redstone (5)

Here are examples of compelling recommendations offered by the Sinsky team:

- *Adding capacity by sharing the care among the team.* In many practices, patients cannot reliably see their own primary care physician the same day a need arises. In addition, most patients are not receiving all recommended prevention and chronic illness care.
- *Solution.* Improving access and increasing adherence to clinical guidelines requires building additional capacity into the practice. Many sites accomplished capacity building by transforming the roles of medical assistants, licensed practical nurses, registered nurses, and health coaches so that they assume partial responsibility for elements of care. In addition, some practices have an extended care team of social workers, behavioralists, nutritionists, and pharmacists, usually working with several clinician–medical assistant teamlets.

  Example 1. At North Shore Physicians Group (NSPG) in the Boston area, the medical assistant's role has been transformed. When a patient is taken to an examination room (rooming), the process has been expanded from three minutes to eight minutes and now includes medication review, agenda setting, form completion, and closing care gaps. For example, the medical assistant reviews health-monitoring reminders, gives immunizations, and proactively books appointments for mammograms and . . . scans for osteoporosis. . . . The role transformation for medical assistants is part of a larger team-care initiative at NSPG, which has resulted in a 14 percent increase in primary care physician satisfaction scores. "We knew our physicians were dissatisfied with the quality of the interaction with the patient because of all the things they had to do in the exam room that was nonphysician work," said Sharon Lucie, vice president for Operations, during an interview (December 11, 2011). "Now providers are begging us to get them started in the new model."

Example 2. Clinica Family Health Services near Denver has created standing orders empowering registered nurses to diagnose and treat simple problems without a physician's involvement. These problems include streptococcal throat infections, conjunctivitis, ear infections, head lice, sexually transmitted diseases, uncomplicated urinary tract infections, and warfarin management.

Example 3. At Clinica Family Health Services, nonprofessional health coaches provide patient education and counseling to help patients with chronic conditions set goals and formulate action plans. Medical assistants sensing depression symptoms administer the nine-item "Patient Health Questionnaire" depression screen and then contact the team's behaviorist.

- *Greater focus on physician satisfaction.* The *Annals of Family Medicine* study is just one sign of growing interest in how to address low physician morale. The research project is funded by the American Board of Internal Medicine Foundation in Philadelphia, which hosted a conference in March 2012 that focused on how workflow innovations could improve the efficiency and appeal of primary care.

We also rely on Jonathan P. Weiner, Susan Yeh, David Blumenthal, "The Impact of Health Information Technology and E-Health on the Future Demand for Physician Services," *Health Affairs* 32(1) (November 4, 2013): 1998–2004, and Atul Gawande, "The Checklist: If Something So Simple Can Transform Intensive Care, What Else Can It Do?," *New Yorker,* December 10, 2007.

CHAPTER 9

At Kaiser Permanente (KP), we rely on Drs. Paul Minardi, Jeff Weisz, Michael Kanter, and Scott Young. Also at KP, we rely on Lisa Schilling, vice president of National Health Care Performance Improvement for KP and director of the KP Performance Improvement Institute; Matt Stiefel, senior director of the Center for Population Health at the Care Management Institute and John August, retired executive director of the Coalition of Kaiser Permanente Unions.

We also rely on Dr. Beth Overbeck at HealthPartners in Minnesota; Drs. Rick Lopez and Kate Koplan at Atrius Health in Massachusetts; Dr. Jim Acton, formerly of Cincinnati Children's Hospital and currently at the University of Missouri Children's Hospital; and Jeanne Weiland from Cincinnati Children's Hospital.

We rely on Committee on Quality of Health Care in America, Institute of Medicine, *Crossing the Quality Chasm: A New Health System for the 21st Century* (Washington, DC: National Academy Press, 2001); M. H. Kanter, O. Martinez, G. Lindsay, and K. Andrews, "Proactive Office Encounter: A Systematic Approach to Preventive and Chronic Care at Every Patient Encounter," *Permanente Journal* 14(3) (2010): 38–43; and M. H. Kanter, G. Lindsay, J. Bellows, and A. Chase, "Complete Care at Kaiser Permanente: Transforming Chronic and Preventive Care," *Joint Commission on Quality and Patient Safety* 39(11) (2013): 484–494; "Kaiser Permanente Case Study: Proactive Office Encounter and Employee Performance Sharing Program; Better Care through Coordinated Teams and Health Information Technology," March 27, 2009, http://xnet.kp.org/future/ahrstudy/032709proactive.html; Alan Whippy et al., "Collaborative Improvement in Sepsis Identification and Treatment—Kaiser Permanente's Performance Improvement System, Part 3: Multisite Improvements in Care for Patients with Sepsis," *Joint Commission Journal* (November 2011); D. Brink, J. Barlow, K. Bush, N. Chaudhary, M. Fareed, R. Hayes, I. Jafri, K. Nair, K. Retzer, and K. Rueter, "Health Care Guidelines: Colorectal Cancer Screening," Institute for Clinical Systems Improvement, May 2012, https://www.icsi.org/_asset/j73fu0/Colorectal.pdf.

CHAPTER 10

We rely on extensive research from Harris Interactive as well as from Dr. Aaron E. Carroll of the Indiana University School of Medicine. We also rely on Dr. Gary Kaplan and Cathie Furman, RN, from Virginia Mason Medical Center, and Dr. Lucian L. Leape, head of the Lucian Leape Institute at the National Patient Safety Foundation. We rely on research from the Commonwealth Fund, reporting from the *Wall Street Journal*, and insights from Tom Emerick, coauthor with Al Lewis of *Cracking Health Costs: How to Cut Your Company's Costs and Provide Employees Better Care* (Hoboken, NJ: Wiley, 2013). In addition, we rely on Christine A. Sinsky, Rachel Willard-Grace, Andrew M. Schutzbank, Thomas A. Sinsky, David Margolius, and Thomas Bodenheimer, "In Search of Joy in Practice: A Report of 23 High-Functioning Primary Care Practices," *Annals of Family Medicine* 11(3) (May–June 2013): 272–278; as well as on Stuart Guterman, "Wielding the Carrot and the Stick: How to Move the U.S. Health Care System Away from Fee-for-Service Payment," The Commonwealth Fund, August 27, 2013, http://www.commonwealthfund.org/Blog/2013/Aug/ Wielding-the-Carrot-and-the-Stick.aspx.

We also rely on Maggie Mahar, "Myths about Medical Malpractice: Part 2, Crisis or Hoax?," HealthBeat Blog, June 30, 2011, http://www.healthbeatblog.com/2011 /06/myths-about-medical-malpractice-part-2-crisis-or -hoax/; We rely on ABC News "Most Doctors will Face Malpractice Suit, AMA says," August 5, 2010, MedPage Today; Aaron E. Carroll, "Malpractice Defense Costs Are Real," The Incidental Economist Blog, April 16, 2012, http://theincidentaleconomist.com/wordpress/malprac tice-defense-costs-are-real/; Stuart Guterman, "Wielding the Carrot and the Stick: How to Move the U.S. Health Care System Away from Fee-for-Service Payment," The Commonwealth Fund Blog, August 27, 2013, http://www.commonwealthfund.org/Blog/2013/Aug/Wielding-the-Carrot-and-the-Stick.aspx; and "Remaking Health Care: Change the Way Providers Are Paid," *Wall Street Journal,* November 19, 2012, http://online.wsj.com/news/articles/SB10001424127887324556304578120450099279338.

Index

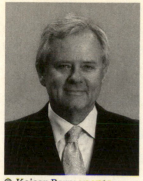

Jack Cochran, MD, FACS, is the executive director of The Permanente Federation, the national umbrella organization for the regional Permanente Medical Groups that comprise the physician component of Kaiser Permanente. The Permanente Medical Groups employ more than 17,000 physicians who care for 9 million Kaiser Permanente members.

Prior to his appointment to The Permanente Federation in October 2007, Dr. Cochran served as executive medical director, president, and chairman of the board of the Colorado Permanente Medical Group (CPMG) for Kaiser Permanente. He began his career with CPMG in 1990 as the chief of plastic surgery and founder of its Plastic Surgery Department.

Dr. Cochran is a frequent speaker and author on a broad range of health care topics, including physician leadership, health information systems, delivery system reform, and integrated care delivery, and his insights gained from decades of work on the front lines of health care provide a unique perspective. He has participated in implementing many of the priorities called for in health reform, including Kaiser Permanente's electronic health record, the largest successful nongovernmental clinical information systems deployment in the world.

Dr. Cochran earned his medical degree from the University of Colorado and served residencies at the Stanford University Medical Center and the University of Wisconsin Hospital. He is board certified in otolaryngology (head and neck surgery) and in plastic and reconstructive surgery.

© Roger Farrington

Charles Kenney is the author of *The Best Practice: How the New Quality Movement Is Transforming Medicine* (2008), which the *New York Times* described as "the first large-scale history of the quality movement." He is the author of *Transforming Health Care: Virginia Mason Medical Center's Pursuit of the Perfect Patient Experience* (2008), for which he was awarded the 2012 Shingo Research and Professional Publication Award. Charlie is also the author (with Maureen Bisognano) of *Pursuing the Triple Aim: Seven Innovators Show the Way to Better Care, Better Health, and Lower Costs* (2012).

For six years, Charles served as a consultant to Blue Cross Blue Shield of Massachusetts on the company's quality initiative. A former journalist, he worked at both the *Boston Globe* and the CBS television affiliate in Boston. Charles currently serves on the faculty of the Institute for Healthcare Improvement.

PublicAffairs is a publishing house founded in 1997. It is a tribute to the standards, values, and flair of three persons who have served as mentors to countless reporters, writers, editors, and book people of all kinds, including me.

I. F. STONE, proprietor of *I. F. Stone's Weekly*, combined a commitment to the First Amendment with entrepreneurial zeal and reporting skill and became one of the great independent journalists in American history. At the age of eighty, Izzy published *The Trial of Socrates*, which was a national bestseller. He wrote the book after he taught himself ancient Greek.

BENJAMIN C. BRADLEE was for nearly thirty years the charismatic editorial leader of *The Washington Post*. It was Ben who gave the *Post* the range and courage to pursue such historic issues as Watergate. He supported his reporters with a tenacity that made them fearless and it is no accident that so many became authors of influential, best-selling books.

ROBERT L. BERNSTEIN, the chief executive of Random House for more than a quarter century, guided one of the nation's premier publishing houses. Bob was personally responsible for many books of political dissent and argument that challenged tyranny around the globe. He is also the founder and longtime chair of Human Rights Watch, one of the most respected human rights organizations in the world.

•   •   •

For fifty years, the banner of Public Affairs Press was carried by its owner Morris B. Schnapper, who published Gandhi, Nasser, Toynbee, Truman, and about 1,500 other authors. In 1983, Schnapper was described by *The Washington Post* as "a redoubtable gadfly." His legacy will endure in the books to come.

Peter Osnos, *Founder and Editor-at-Large*